getting
organized
to enjoy
more time,
space and
freedom in
your home

Orderly
PLACES

Mary Frances Ballard

MORGAN JAMES PUBLISHING • NEW YORK

Orderly PLACES

by Mary Frances Ballard

ISBN: 978-1-60037-684-9 (Paperback)

Library of Congress Control Number: 2009932871

Published by:

MORGAN · JAMES
THE ENTREPRENEURIAL PUBLISHER ™
www.morganjamespublishing.com

Morgan James Publishing, LLC
1225 Franklin Ave. Ste 325
Garden City, NY 11530-1693
Toll Free 800-485-4943
www.MorganJamesPublishing.com

Cover/Interior Design by:
Rachel Lopez
rachel@r2cdesign.com

Photography by:
Karen Woodward, *The Container Store*

Author Photo by: Joe Fudge

In an effort to support local communities, raise awareness and funds, Morgan James Publishing donates one percent of all book sales for the life of each book to Habitat for Humanity.
Get involved today, visit **www.HelpHabitatForHumanity.org.**

DEDICATION

To my Mother,
a brilliant and Godly woman
who in her shortened life
taught me not only organizing principles
but by her example how to walk humbly before the Lord.

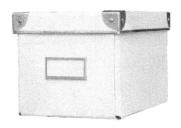

CONTENTS

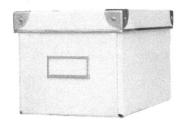

ACKNOWLEDGEMENTS

THE STORIES SHARED HERE are from my experiences as a professional organizer with clients from many backgrounds, occupations, ages and income levels. Their names and some specifics have been changed to protect their privacy. In many instances they have become my friends and I enjoy maintaining contact with them. Without their input, this manuscript could have been simply a dry reference book with no life. I thank each of them.

I am blessed to have many who encouraged me to write this book and helped in the final product. They are: colleagues and friends from my former career as an educator, my church congregation, the Colonial Piecemakers Quilting Guild, my organizing peers and my encouraging family. I am grateful to all of them including these who helped with editing: Sally Burri, Karen DiMarino, Debra Dunn, Mary Gill, Evelyn Stone and Mary Tatem.

The Container Store, with locations all over the country and online, provided photographs of great organizing products, and Karen Woodward created the graphics of the filing solutions. These have made the book much more interesting and informative.

Margo Toulouse and the staff at Morgan James Publishing were very supportive, instructive and accommodating in this process. Their professionalism and assistance was essential and is much appreciated.

Special thanks go to Don Aslett and his wonderful books on organizing and other things that have kept me inspired, motivated and entertained for more than 25 years.

And last but not least, as they say, my most heartfelt thanks go to my one and only husband, Eddie, who has always given me whatever I have wanted including his support with this book.

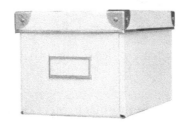

INTRODUCTION

THEY SAY NOTHING TASTES as good as being thin feels. I haven't been able to verify that theory lately, but I can tell you that being disorganized does not feel as good as being organized with more time in your day and freedom in the space in your home or office.

There is a deep seated desire in our spirits, souls and bodies to be free. We are encouraged to live a healthy lifestyle so our bodies can be free from disease. Patrick Henry declared the necessity of political freedom with his, "Give me liberty or give me death" outcry. Beth Moore encourages us to exercise our spiritual freedom in her book, *Breaking Free*. We want to be free from debt, free to walk our city streets without harm, free to vote and free to come and go as we please.

But very few on Wall Street or Main Street are encouraging us to be free from things. Our schedules and homes are so full that we are overwhelmed with decisions on how to spend our time and what to do with our things. We are yearning to be free.

Most of us need a plan to get organized. Whether you are attempting organizing for the first time, you need only specific areas to organize or you need a plan to keep what you have maintained, the strategies here will help you.

The process for organizing is given in a logical sequence and specific areas are covered in separate chapters.

Of course I think reading the book from cover to cover is the best method, but some of you may first choose to read the areas that are most appropriate to you. Just like there are many styles to organizing, there are many ways to read this book.

While organizing is not a humorous subject, I have tried to lighten it up with whatever warped sense of humor I have left after a teaching career in the middle schools. My surgeon once told me I should have a psychiatric exam after every teaching term. Most of this humor is at my expense.

As you read through these pages, it is my hope that you will see the situations in your space and schedules with a new perspective, that you will be able to use the information to be better organized, and as a result you will be free—free to use and be happy with the things and spaces in your homes and free to have more time to enjoy your relationships with others even more.

Your comments, questions or personal organizing stories are important to me. I also enjoy speaking to business, community or church organizations. Contact me through e-mail: maryfrances@orderlyplaces.com, or my website: www.orderlyplaces.com. Your personal information will always remain confidential.

PART ONE
The Problems in Organizing

Chapter 1

WHAT IS IN OUR SPACES AND SCHEDULES?

t he lawn at Andrea's house was green and manicured, the shrubs trimmed and a few bunches of blooming flowers greeted me as I entered the home. Inside was a different story. The dining room table was layered with stacks of old newspapers, magazines, purchases from local stores still in their bags, craft projects for the Boys Scouts and piles of mail, old and new.

And that was just the beginning. Every room was bulging with stuff. Toys were scattered around the edges of toy boxes, clothing was jammed into closets and drawers, and there was no room to walk in the garage much less contain a vehicle.

Was this the home of a non-caring parent, a lazy adult or an overworked single mom? No, this was an upper middle class family that simply had so many misplaced things and was overwhelmed with what to do with all of it.

Andrea not only had a house full of too many things, but her schedule was packed with responsibilities. She was a part time educator, a wife and mother of young boys, a scout troop leader, a neighborhood watch liaison, a garden club member, etc.

Like many of us, she was very talented and gifted in so many ways that she was often called on to help out in many capacities. Being the generous and accommodating soul that she was, it was almost impossible to turn down requests to assist or even lead others in their activities. She was committed to doing too many things and she didn't know how to make her schedule better.

OUR SPACES AND THINGS NOW

Have you ever become frustrated because you could not put your hands on a receipt you needed? Is there ever a hunt for a child's missing shoe or the car keys as you get ready to leave in the morning? And what about that bill that needs to be paid and you can't remember where you saved it? Trust me, you are not alone and I speak from experience. Those scenarios play over and over across the country every day and yes some have been taken from the pages of my life.

Many of us can relate to the dilemma of not knowing where to put the things we have collected over the years. In our affluence, we have so much that we assume a bigger house with lots of walk in closets, a 2 or 3 car garage, a bigger basement or attic, or as last resort a rented storage facility will fix the problem. I have found this not to be so in my visits to homes small and large, old and new, maintained and neglected.

WHAT HAPPENED TO OUR HOMES?

The world and especially America has changed drastically since the post war era when I was born. I grew up in a custom built home, small but considered sufficient for that generation. My sister and I shared a bedroom with a 3 foot wide closet and a chest that had 4 drawers. It held all of our clothes, toys, games and other personal belongings. It also hid our cat when we wanted to bring it in the house without our parents knowing about it. We even dressed that poor thing in our doll's clothes. (PETA, I have reformed.)

Today that space would hardly hold the clothes of one child, much less the countless other possessions. We have been convinced by the bombardment of stimuli in many forms that we need more things. While I applaud capitalism and enjoy the wonderful advances in our quality of life, accumulating more and more things has brought on a new set of challenges.

Our Schedules Now

Our daily lives have become flooded with more and more things to do but we are not doing those things we really would love to do. We want to avail ourselves of every opportunity out there for growth, leisure, motivation, inspiration, etc. And we want all of that for our children, too. In our effort to excel, we have multi-tasked ourselves into a revolving door that seems to have no end.

It is not uncommon for a mom to prepare herself and her children for a day away from home at work and school and never get back there until evening hours when the chauffeuring and errands are completed. We have convinced ourselves that no opportunity should be missed that could broaden our lives or that of our children. In doing so we have lost the greatest opportunity of all, that of spending time building relationships in our families. There will never be more than 24 hours in our days but we have overscheduled them as if there were no tomorrow.

What Happened to our Schedules?

As our physical lives have become crowded with things, our schedules have become crowded with obligations, responsibilities and opportunities that our forefathers could never have dreamed. The modernization of our lifestyles has given us more time away from the menial tasks of our grandparents but at the same time it has left us with an emptiness and inner drive to do more.

We are obligated to support our families and have responsibilities in caring for them, but we have engaged in opportunities far beyond the basic things needed to provide an adequate and satisfying lifestyle.

In fact, we are not content with adequate but want to do more and more for others as well as ourselves. There is no end to the educational, musical, physical, social and spiritual classes, courses, groups and opportunities for us to join. And it is so hard to choose which are best for our children and us individually. We over commit our time and find ourselves exhausted at the end of every day without having done what we really wanted to do.

Future Generations

Every parent wants their children to learn more, earn more and have more than they have experienced. That is human nature. And we have set the example for them ourselves by stretching every resource we have to accumulate and do all of those things. What we have not learned is that more of those things have often led to more debt, more stress, more mess, and more frustration and less freedom.

Our budgets are straining and our spaces simply cannot contain in an orderly manner what we now own. Our schedules are filled to overflowing and we don't have the time to build relationships with those we love because are doing so many things.

We are prisoners in the problem of what to do to correct these situations. We need freedom to live comfortably and orderly in our spaces and freedom to enjoy the time we have with our loved ones as well as the activities in our schedules.

Is Help is on the Way?

It is not surprising that television programs, magazine articles and other books on organizing, decluttering, redesigning spaces, planning our day, our meals and our entertainment have become so popular in the last few years. (Even I get inspired with *Clean Sweep, Mission Organization, Martha Stewart* and *Rachel Ray*.) In addition a relatively new career, professional organizing, has come on the scene. We are professionals who provide individuals with assistance and training in strategies that create order in the house and time in our day.

Now we have new sections in department and discount stores devoted exclusively to organizing products, and specialty stores are available now that carry only containers and other organizing supplies. All of these are to help us better control the things in our homes.

There are more courses on time management than there is time to take them and more styles of calendars, planners, notepads, blackberries, blueberries, or whatever berries, etc. than one could use in a lifetime of planning. But they have not solved our over scheduling dilemma.

We must admit we are smothered by our many things and activities and we need to get set free. We need to get organized. The purpose of this book is to help you get organized in your spaces and schedules and enjoy the freedom that brings.

The Solution Begins in Our Heads

One of the most frequent features couples look for a new home today is how much storage space is available. Bigger is not always better and it is not the answer to better organization. More hours in a day would give us time but for what? It might help for a little while, but the same problems will manifest themselves over again in the new space or schedule. Why?

Lack of organization is not a space or time problem, it is a head problem.

Think About It ···

Think about the space you have now. Unless you have downsized from your previous home, you probably had adequate space when you first moved in. Like the Field of Dreams, the empty spaces began to be filled until now there may be just too much stuff for the space.

The same is true of time. You have always had the same amount of hours in your day but there seems to be less now. The older you get, the more you try to cram in each day as if it may be your last or you might miss out on something good. It is hard for you to stop filling each block of time with another activity and yet you are not reaching those goals you set for yourselves.

Obviously an expanding family requires more time and space and babies have their own demands like no one else in the family. We will discuss those concerns and the challenges children bring to the equation in later chapters.

We cannot blame them, however, for all of the organizational problems in the home. After all, they haven't even learned how to use those 36 shapes of cookie cutters or the melon ball shaper or how to use the remote as we sit in a fog switching channels all evening. (And we won't even mention the items in the most sacred of places—the garage.) Well, yes we will mention it. After all, how many flat head screwdrivers does it take to change a light bulb?

Chapter 2

WHAT IS ORGANIZING?

he definition of being organized means different things to different people. We each have our own organizing personalities just as we differ in learning styles, talents and skills. But there are basic organizing principles and strategies that work for everyone, and likewise there are common problems that can keep any of us from being organized.

We live in a world that was created with orderly systems. It is so orderly that we set our clocks by it and send men into space with precision timing. Gravity always works, and unfortunately it sometimes proves itself in our bodies.

We have an inborn desire to be orderly, too. Normal babies learn specific developmental tasks in a given sequence. They learn to say, "No" before "Yes" which we are now discovering is a good thing and are rehearsing again as adolescence approaches--"Just say NO". We develop routines that are comfortable to us, and we enjoy spaces that accommodate our lifestyles in an orderly fashion.

Regardless of your personality, intelligence, income, talents, race or religion, I believe you were created by an orderly God to be an orderly person and you will never be content until you can see that fulfilled in your life. Order brings peace and stability to the most humble or the most ostentatious environments and freedom to our lives

ORGANIZING IS POSSIBLE.

When spaces are organized, items can be located within a minute, every item has a permanent and specific home, there are not too many items in any one space, and one can move about and use things efficiently and safely.

If there is order in our spaces, there is a much better chance for our schedules to be organized because time is not lost dealing with things. Lost items, misplaced items, missing items and items in the way require more upkeep and attention and steal our time

It could be the Shakers had it figured out with their simple way of ordering their homes. I have often thought that if I could start my married life over I would use their décor as a guide for mine. The rooms had simple furnishings with quilts, a few other textiles and baskets as the decorations. With so much less in the room they were safe and orderly places that were much easier to maintain. I doubt they wasted time looking for things.

Organizing is a learned skill and behavior. Finding what organizing systems work for you may take some time and energy, some challenging decision making and some lifestyle changes, but it is possible to be successful at it. I am living proof of that.

Confession Time

Being a left brain and more logical personality, I think I have always been organized in my head. Even in college I made my bed every morning and kept my desk cleared so I could study without distraction.

But as a busy young mother with three children, two dogs (and various other short lived pets) and responsibilities at church and in the community, I allowed my schedule and things to accumulate in our home to the point where there was considerable clutter.

We are talking about lots of stuff and I was responsible for most of it. (Not all of it because we did have a garage at every house we lived in.) But I did have lots of hobbies and "collections". I was a home economics and education major in college which means I had 3 hours credit here and maybe 6 hours there on topics all related to home and housing. In other words, I graduated a jack of all trades and master of none. This created an interest in all kinds of things including craft projects and collecting of nostalgia. It also meant I could help others with lots of projects that took lots of my time.

Binging on Things

Some of you may remember macramé plant hangers, fabric flowers, painted skirts and stenciled hand towels. The country's bicentennial celebration came along with quilting, basket weaving and decorative pottery. Finally, I tried my hand at tole painting followed by watercolors.

And we are not done yet. There was the collecting of tin canisters, Precious Moments figurines, folk art angels and antique sewing notions and equipment. At one time I had a treadle sewing machine that we used as a lamp stand for lack of space for it.

The dining room was fondly called the Bermuda Triangle because once things went in there, they were rarely found again. (I think I mentioned another dining room table earlier. They are just too convenient for stuff.) Although that room was already crowded with a table, computer desk, china cabinet and large buffet, there was one corner vacant but not for long.

Camping Gone Astray

When my children were too young to know their parents were boring, we took them camping. Behind our 9 passenger station wagon (forerunner of the mini van) we pulled a pop up camper. On one summer weekend we went to the Shenandoah Valley to spend time at a lakeside campground.

While the kids were busy I took a trip to see the local scenery and found a great Hoosier cabinet for sale in an old barn. Later when I talked with my husband about buying it he asked where I would put it. My answer for that question was always, "I will make a space for it." The Lord knows there was precious little vacant space in that house, but I remembered the only empty corner in the dining room.

You might think that is the end of the story, but remember we were camping. My obsession with collecting even more stuff forced us to put some luggage in the camper, some packages on the carrying rack on top of the car and that tall cabinet in the back of the station wagon.

In order to accommodate it, we had to fold down all the seats but the bench in the front. Since there were seatbelts for three in there, the youngest of the three children sat between my husband and me and the other two were stuffed prone on each side of the cabinet on the 3 hour trip home. At least they could not be seen not wearing a seat belt.

Even with lots of stuff I was internally driven to be organized so I tried shuffling the things in the house around hoping it would look and function better. We all know how that was working for me.

DIFFERENT STROKES (ORDER) FOR DIFFERENT FOLKS

Your personality may be more right brain, creative and abstract allowing things to literally fall into place as you go about your business. And so you might assume that you will never be able to get or stay organized. The exact opposite is true. While your spaces may not look like everyone else's and your systems are very different, you can improve your situation.

Donna enjoyed doing her paperwork at her kitchen table although there was a nice office in her home. Unfortunately the calendars, notepads, etc. were always in the way at mealtime. We created a storage area for her supplies in a rolling cart that could be pulled away from the wall and over to the kitchen table when she was ready to use it. When it was time to eat, the cart was moved back to its home against the wall. While some might think she should have moved her paperwork to the home office, that was not her preference.

Organizing does not always look the same for everyone but it is possible for everyone to be organized.

ORGANIZING AS A GIFT

Incredibly, God believes in organization as a gift. Trust me on this. In the Old Testament, II Kings 20:1 the prophet tells the king to put his house in order because tomorrow he will die. Any of you who have had to clear the estate of a deceased packrat can appreciate that verse of wisdom.

My father lived through the Great Depression and saved everything from books to bolts and silver coins to shirts (dozens still in original packaging). As my sisters and I sorted through his things after his death, I promised myself and my family that I would never put my children through that experience. It is physically, mentally and emotionally exhausting, not to mention time consuming. It was never his intent to burden us in that way but what little bit of cleaning out he would do from time to time was insufficient to take care of his lifetime habit of consuming and saving things.

EXITING INSTRUCTIONS

While you are still in your right mind, take care of your exiting instructions. In addition to our Last Will and Testament, my husband and I continually evaluate and purge our possessions. We also have written notes on how our less costly possessions should be divided.

Our children are grown with families of their own so we asked them what they would like to have that is in our home. They prioritized their list and we sorted through them so that each one would get what he wanted most. (I could hardly believe that no one asked for my fabric stash, so I requested that it be left to my quilting guild.) As much as you are able, take care of the decisions now that need to be made with your things when you are gone.

Give the gift of an orderly place and freedom from hard decisions to your survivors. They will love you and thank you now and when you are gone.

Organizing Evaluations.

The following is a survey I created that lists many common areas of concern when trying to organize spaces and ultimately time. Most of us are challenged in some areas but very few of us would be challenged in all of them. In completing it, you need to take an honest look at your present behaviors and habits.

At the end is a summary of what your score may reveal about your organizing lifestyle. If you would like further descriptions of organizing behaviors, The National Study Group on Chronic Disorganization has Fact Sheets and a clutter-hoarding scale available at their website, www.nsgcd.org

[ORGANIZATION SURVEY]

Answer the following questions on a scale from 0 to 3 as follows:

0 – Never **1 – Sometimes** **2 – Usually** **3 - Always**

0 –None **1 – Some (1-2)** **2 – Several (3-4)** **3 – Many (5-6)**

Give a zero for those that do not apply to you or your home.

Total your score.

1. If I walk through my house in the dark, I may trip over something. ____

2. I waste time looking for my keys before I leave the house. ____

3. Mail piles up for several days or turns yellow before sorting. ____

4. I have magazines over one month old and possibly never read. ____

5. I have catalogues over 1 month old and I have indoor plumbing. ____

6. I have newspapers over 1 week old and I am not housebreaking a dog. ____

7. I waste time looking for important papers when I need them. ____

8. I have items stacked on my desk or work area. ____

9. My bookcase is too full and I don't have time to read. ____

10. My clothes are packed tightly in my closet. ____

11. My clothing drawers are full or overflowing. ____

12. I leave unfinished projects spread out overnight. ____

13. I do not have time to make my bed in the morning. ____

14. I have an overflowing clothes hamper. ____

15. There are clothes on the floor. ____

16. I have clothing needing repair for more than a month. ____

17. I have clothing I have not worn for at least one year. ____

18. I waste time trying to find my toiletries or cosmetics in the morning. ____

19. I have run out of toilet paper in at least one bathroom. ____

20. I have kitchen tools or utensils I have not used in a year. ____

21. I have cookbooks I have not used in a year. ____

22. My refrigerator has leftovers stored for more than 1 week. ____

23. I panic if visitors are coming unexpectedly. ____

24. I feel I deny myself if I don't take advantage of "sales". ____

25. I buy several items if I see "Buy one get one free". ____

26. I buy items at garage sales/thrift shops, etc. that are not on a "needs" list. ____

27. I have "collections" that I do not display neatly or enjoy. ____

28. I have a collection of items to "re-gift". ____

29. There are tapes or videos or CD's that no one has used in 1 year. ____

30. There are stacks of books, papers, magazines on the floor or seating areas. ____

31. When I stop my car suddenly, items fall on the floor. ____

32. There are phone books that are not the most current. ____

33. I own art, pictures or photos that are not displayed or sorted properly. ____

34. I waste time trying to find what I need in my files. ____

35. I waste time trying to locate warranties, guarantees, instruction manuals, etc. ____

36. I have missed payments because of misplaced bills. ____

37. I cannot locate stationery items I know I have. ____

38. I neglect balancing my checking account with the monthly statement. ____

39. The dog can find things faster than I can. ____

40. It takes more than 5 minutes to straighten up a room before I can clean it. ____

41. I run out of cleaning/laundry supplies unexpectedly. ____

42. The hobby/craft storage is messy. ____

43. The garage/storage shed is cluttered. ____

44. The attic is unorganized/cluttered. ____

45.	The stored items are not labeled.	____
46.	I save things for fear I may need them someday.	____
47.	I save things I do not like just because they were gifts.	____
48.	I save things because I spent a lot of money on them.	____
49.	I think I need a bigger house with more storage space.	____
50.	I think I need to organize my time better than I do.	____

TOTAL = ____

IF YOU SCORED ZERO, you may close this book and write one of your own. You have obviously gained control of the spaces and time in your life.

A SCORE OF 1-20 indicates a high level of organization with good habits. Any areas of concern may be temporary but if not, you probably have the skills to deal with them.

A SCORE OF 21-50 is satisfactory. While you may have control of some areas, there is room for improvement and taking action will improve your situation.

A SCORE OF 51-75 is livable but of concern. Without taking steps to find solutions for some of the problem areas, frustration and stress could affect your daily life.

A SCORE OF 76 and higher indicates problems in several areas which can lead to even more areas falling into disorganization. Some lifestyle behaviors and habits need to be changed in order to create a better environment for everyone.

Chapter 3

WHAT IF YOU ARE DISORGANIZED?

do you hesitate to have guests in your home because of the mess that is there? Do you have to move piles to sit down or begin work on a project? Do you have inherited items with no place to put them? Are you renting a storage unit for your excess items? Have you ever thought, "This space has always been a problem for me? I have rearranged it over and over but I just can't keep it organized." Perhaps you have unpacked boxes or bags with purchases still in them because you don't know where to begin placing the items.

A breakdown in orderly environments is called disorganization. There can be many causes for this and we will discuss each one in more detail. Do not feel defeated or hopeless because you have found yourself frustrated or overwhelmed at your surroundings or schedule. We will discuss organizing your spaces first and then give strategies to manage your schedules in later chapters. Regardless of the cause there is always hope and the situation can turn around. You can have success and feel free in your time and space.

Considering Changes

In reading this book, you have already considered the possibility that your present organizing strategies with spaces and schedules need help. Your concerns may be correct if you have trouble finding things, if you have too many things for the space you have, if there are piles of unsorted things, if you are storing things you do not like or if you keep things out of guilt or fear of what the future may bring. If your schedule is overwhelming then you probably want changes there too.

On the other hand, you may have your spaces or schedules under control except for a few rooms in your home or times in your day and you are looking for solutions to help with those. Either situation can be improved by taking an honest look at the reasons behind what caused things to be in their present condition. You will have to look honestly at your situation to see it and make some changes to improve it.

The Rest of the Story

If I could be set free from clutter, then so can you. An organizational turn around took place with me when I read two books by Don Aslett in the mid 1980's. The first book was *Is Their Life After Housework?* If you think about all the stuff I had you can imagine what house cleaning was like. I saw the ad for that book, ordered it, devoured it and showed it to my friend, Jane, who was also ready to make a change.

Now you have to remember that this was before the Swifter mop and Pledge dust wipes. The book had instructions on using janitorial supplies to properly clean a house. So Jane and I made our list from the book suggestions and drove the station wagon down into the "warehouse" section of town.

We had to crawl up onto the loading dock to get into the supply house, but in our preppy little tab front shirts (not that little) with alligators on the pockets, we proceeded to ask for Ettore Steccone squeegees, 11 x 17 masslin cloths, deluxe extension handles to go with the 18" cotton dust mops with rotating handles (which I still love today), dry sponges chemically treated, plus liquid cleaners, not one but two 3" x 5" olefin mats with vinyl backing (very ugly but necessary at the entrances) etc. until we finished the list.

Words cannot express the looks we were getting from the staff as they brought us our things. You would have thought we were from a TV stunt show or dropped down from Mars. We paid our bill, loaded up the station wagon, hopped in the front seat and laughed with tears streaming all the way home.

I was happy to have a cleaning system and Jane bartered off her cleaning talents with friends who would wallpaper her kitchen or weed her flower beds for a concrete seal on their garage floor.

Clutter's Last Stand

A couple of years later I got a flyer in the mail advertising Don's (oh yes, I was on first name basis now) next book, *Clutter's Last Stand*. He had quit preaching and started meddling. It became very clear that many of my housekeeping problems were related to the clutter (hobbies, collections and more).

There was a paradigm shift in my thinking about my things. I wanted to be free from trying to keep them in order, but like many of you I was unsure if I was really willing to let them go. Step by step and over time, I made the decisions and changes needed. In fact, it is a continuing process even today.

Home Staging

Not long after reading that book, I began a short career in real estate. During that time I had some good organizational training at a seminar by

Barbara Swartz, the guru of home staging. I was hooked and began to read, learn and apply even more principles that all professional organizers now use.

Since I loved the results so much, I continued using those learned skills to help others. Over time I found a new freedom from attachments to things and more space in my environment and schedule. I joined several organizing groups including the National Association of Professional Organizers, Faithful Organizers and the National Study Group on Chronic Disorganization. The rest is history.

MAKING ORGANIZING WORK FOR YOU

Some organizing problems are related to the way things are arranged in the space or schedule. You put the items where you think you will be able to use them efficiently but later find out they are always in the way of what you are doing or they are not close enough to be convenient. It is not necessarily that there is too much to handle. This may be an organizing system that doesn't match your lifestyle.

Or perhaps you have planned your day and interruptions upset the way you wanted things to go, people around you changed what you wanted to do, or you just could not keep up with what you planned.

After a few sessions of trial and error you may have become frustrated and given up on trying to figure out what to do to improve the situation. As we go through the organizing steps in the next section, I will explain a process to use that will help you find an orderly arrangement for your things and schedules.

• Personality and Preferences

As already mentioned certain personality types have a more casual attitude towards organization and others have organizing preferences that might appear to be contrary to what others might consider the normal or "right" way to arrange things or your day.

There is no such thing as a right or wrong way to organize. Each person is unique, each environment is different and every space and schedule can be arranged to accommodate the situation. Personality type is never a valid excuse for staying disorganized.

• Life Happens

Besides your own organizing personality, keeping things and your day in order may be more difficult as the seasons of your life change. These usually occur around significant events such as these.

Birth of a baby

Catastrophic or terminal illness in the family

Death of a loved one,

Divorce

Children leaving for college or marriage

Changes in job situations

Moving

Bankruptcy

Accidents

Retirement

Some less significant events can also change your lifestyle temporarily.

Holidays

Guests arriving

Vacations

Renovating your home

Special occasions or celebrations

During these times, being organized may become a very difficult challenge and one simply may not be able to maintain the standards of organization that had been in place.

Mandy is a beautiful young wife and mother who's husband is in the military. He is often deployed for months at a time. Soon after they were married, he was transferred across the country. They bought a house upon their arrival on the east coast, but before the unpacking could be completed, she was put on bed rest for several months to safe guard her pregnancy.

Unpacking was delayed, the husband went on short deployments so little was done to complete or to maintain organization. Then the newborn arrived with all of his demands. More delays and a long term deployment to the Middle East left Mandy with disorganization in many areas of her house. The good news is that her situation has stabilized, we were able to get her back on track, and now she is good to go again.

Life has its ups and downs. Being able to stay positive when all around you seems to be falling apart is an important life strategy. When the situation calms and you can fall back into normal routines, you will be free to resume the organizational systems you once had.

• Don't Blame Mom and Dad

You may think disorganization is an inherited trait and there is no hope for you because one or both of your parents were disorganized. While DNA does contribute to the preferences in the brain, there is no conclusive evidence that there is an organizational chromosome. That is not yet.

In looking at my three children, I believe there is clear evidence otherwise. One is a "neatnik" who lined up his socks in the drawer by age 10. He is still very organized over 20 years later. The other two evidently missed that chromosome and yet they came from the same gene pool, grew up in the same house, went to the same schools and ate the same foods. Go figure.

I am just waiting for the latest research to identify that organizing chromosome's number but until it is found you cannot blame your heredity for your organizational problems

• Life History

Life history, however, can influence your organizing behaviors and lead to disorganization. But you can get over it and move on. Some clients have grown up with disorder all around them, they learned to get used to it and they have put off changing what now is their own problem.

On the other hand, some have rebelled against the spotless home of their youth and now that they are free from it they are determined to let disorganization abound as an act of independence.

Neither reaction will be satisfying over time. Unless there are emotional issues associated with your childhood lifestyle, you can learn organizing strategies that will enable you to make your present home organized and efficient and use your time more effectively and efficiently.

• Emotions are Real

Perhaps you realize that you have some deep seated emotional problems that are hindering your success in many areas including being organized. These need to be evaluated by professionals that can help you address those areas in order to find success.

Fortunately such individuals are not in the majority of disorganized homes but if you are unsure there are resources for help in the resource section.

• Attachments and Sentiment

Disorganization can occur when there are emotional attachments to so many things in the space. Sentiment can cause us to keep things we do not like or want but feel guilty about letting go. They might have belonged to someone we loved deeply who is no longer with us. In letting go of any of their possessions or things that remind us of them, we fear we will lose the person all over again.

Susan had lost Alfred, her husband and the love of her life, to cancer. While in the Air Force, they had traveled the world collecting beautiful items from many countries. Her home was filled with memorabilia from her life with him. Now she needed to downsize to a condo that demanded no yard work and little maintenance.

Her children did not want her things but she could not bear to part with the gifts that Alfred had bought for her. It was very difficult for her to separate her love for Alfred from those things.

It takes courage and thoughtful consideration to be able to separate our loved ones from their things. But they (and we) are not things and when we realize we still have memories of our loved ones with or without things, letting go can be easier.

• Fears About Things

Another strong emotion that influences disorganization is the fear of not having all of our things forever. The "just in case I need them" or "what if I let it go and then I need it" scenario can stall any organizing process. And then there is the "as soon as I got rid of it I needed it" excuse for never letting go of anything again. The root of each of these stumbling blocks is fear. Freedom from it is like a bird being released from its cage.

There is the basic fear that once an item is gone it can never be found or purchased again. This might be true with rare antiques but With Wal-Mart opened 24-7 in nearly every community in America, we would be hard pressed not to be able to replace anything practical we will ever need. And if we fear we won't have the resources to get it again, then we need to be reassured of how we have managed in the past.

Those who have lived through the hard economic times have memories of being without basic needs and they have passed on those fears to the following generations. In our affluence, we need to consider our personal situation and not be controlled by what has happened to our forefathers.

• Fears About Activities

Fears also spill over into our schedules because we are afraid we will miss an opportunity that will never come along again. I have found that the most useful classes, courses, seminars, groups, teams, etc are offered over and over again in one venue or another. When organizing our time most effectively, we may need to postpone some activities until a later date.

Over the years I have observed that we are resourceful people with tremendous abilities to make do with what we have on hand. Rather than being bound by the past, we can look ahead with confidence that all of our needs will be met plus most of our wants.

- ## Belief Systems

This leads right into considering what we really believe about ourselves and being organized. If you engage in negative self talk and believe you cannot be organized then it will be difficult for you to move forward. Do you have strong beliefs about the roles of your family members in getting your home in order? Do you believe disorganization in your home is everyone else's fault? Any of these beliefs can hinder progress.

It is important that you give careful consideration to what you think is possible in your situation. Negative beliefs can be turned around when you see progress and you can be motivated, inspired, and free to continue the process with hope.

- ## Procrastination

Most of us have been guilty of putting off things that need to be done. Making a habit of not dealing with things on a regular basis can result in clutter and disorganization

In my business, the most common types of procrastination I see are the those whose schedules are so full and who commit so much of their time to others that there is no time left to deal with their stuff. I also see those who are afraid to get started in organizing because it may not turn out like what they wanted. They may have a vision but are hesitant for fear of failing.

- ## Don't Fall for the Stall

Linda, a client who is still very dear to me, is a brilliant and goal oriented gal. She is a military officer that moved into the area but had waited 18 months to finish unpacking. Her office at work was immaculate and she could quote from the organizing books. She had a vision of what she wanted the space to look like and had put off unpacking because she wasn't sure how to start and get it right. The assistance of a professional organizer to give her a system and keep her motivated was all she needed to get the job done.

Some of my clients keep waiting for the perfect timing or the right helpers to get started on a project, but once the job is underway they are usually motivated to continue with the systems.

Jan Marie has a home based business that operates from a front room next to the family dining room. The dining room table is not normally used for family meals so its large horizontal surface is inviting to the overflow from the business. When she is expecting visitors, the rush is on to get it cleared and the space presentable. But after the company has gone, she falls back into her old habits. She has a good system that works, but it requires daily maintenance as customers, orders and supplies come in. Unfortunately she procrastinates in keeping it orderly until the next call from visitors coming to town.

Regardless of what type of procrastinator you may be, putting off organizing will only delay having order in your space. Why not be free to enjoy the use of it now?

• Media Influences

The role of the media cannot be ignored in all of this. We are bombarded all day long with enticements to get the new and improved version of what we already have or something new we had not yet considered buying.

Gene Roddenberry of Star Wars fame has reminded us that television does not exist to educate, inform or entertain us. Its purpose is to make money for its owners, and we are proof that its goal is working. If the 7 minute interruption in our favorite program is not enough, there are infomercials that can captivate us for 30 minutes at a time. For the hard core, there are the 24 hour channels that exist simply to entice us with item after item at their special prices.

Before making that call to purchase any item advertised, take the time to check out the reviews for that item in as many sources as you have available. You may be as surprised as I have been at the negative comments about the products.

Right now the media is winning the game of stealing our time and filling our spaces.

• Keeping up with the Jones Family

Even our peers are showing off what now outdates our previously purchased items and we feel deprived. We are pressured to buy what we really don't need but now want. We hear new styles and colors, so called new and improved products call our names, and we become victims of our own insecurities.

The result is we are making purchases that now fill our home to overflowing. Trying to find a place to keep all of that stuff becomes a greater and greater challenge.

That same Jones family will interrupt our schedules with invitations we feel compelled to accept or interruptions we have not prepared to resist. We want to be included and not outcasts in all of the local social events and activities, but we have a hard time choosing what is most important in planning our time.

We are disorganized, we know it but we don't know what to do. We have seen the enemy and we are it.

• Getting Out of the Rut

Being trapped in a disorderly environment or schedule that hinders who you want to be and what you need and want to do is not being free. None of us enjoy making changes to our habits and lifestyle. We get in comfortable ruts and want to stay there until something or someone comes along that inspires or motivates us to change.

If staying organized is difficult you need to think about ineffective lifestyle behaviors or habits that may need changing. Learning the principles and skills involved in organizing can help you with those changes.

As you contemplate the organizing journey there are attributes that will facilitate your success: being open to change, being willing to learn and being ready to begin the change process. The following chapter will give you a starting point in the search for freedom and in creating organized spaces that are both functional and attractive and schedules that are realistic.

PART TWO
Solutions for Organizing Any Space

Chapter 4

THE STARTING POINT

have you picked up a stack of papers to sort and set it down again because you didn't know where to start? Or maybe you have held an item in your hand and looked around for a place to put it and just gave up. Do you just feel overwhelmed and don't know where or how to begin in getting organized?

DECISION MAKING 101

Organizing is the process of making decisions about the things you have. You make a decision whenever you receive a gift but choose to bury it, you make a decision if you choose to buy an item, you make decisions on what to do with what you own, and you make a decision if you get rid of anything.

Soon after I officially began organizing as a business for profit (I use that word loosely), I developed the 5 P's of Orderly Places. They are the steps of decision making I would ask the client to take as we began working together. In summary they are:

Priorities: identifying and giving preference to the important things, spaces, time, etc.

Principles: applying proven organizing methods to create spaces that function and are attractive and schedules that are realistic and effective

Planning: evaluating the spaces, schedules, tools and supplies needed to be organized

Processes: applying strategies, systems and products that are appropriate

Places: knowing and using the resources for information, supplies and assistance as you organize

In the next few chapters we will discuss each one of these steps in more detail. The first several chapters are about our spaces. The remaining chapters are about our time. Some of us have personalities that will be able to make quick decisions and move on. Others require more time to think about things before deciding what to do.

The steps given here allow for both types and it is important that you deliberate on each one in order to have success. For small projects like a drawer, these steps may only take a couple of hours; but for larger spaces more time and thought is needed.

Skipping steps often means having to go back after a project is finished and starting over.

Organizing is an art as well as a science but it can be learned and with practice you can get really good at it. You will be pleased with your skills and you will feel the freedom of new found space and time.

Chapter 5

IDENTIFYING THE PRIORITIES

Priorities are the ways we demonstrate what is important to us. They are formed from our values and goals and are the basis of every decision we make whether consciously or subconsciously. These are developed throughout our lives as we respond to what we learn. They are the result of what we believe in the deepest part of our being and we are most content when we can apply them to every area of our lives including our spaces and schedules.

THE MOST IMPORTANT THINGS

If you have never given serious time and thought to what is really important to you, I would challenge you to do it now. The process can clear up the fog in your thinking processes and give you new freedom in the decision making process. The results can be the foundation for many choices you face and improve the outcome of the many decisions you have to make

- Make a list of the things you would like to do before you die and pick out the top ten.

- Consider how you want to be remembered.

- Write your obituary or eulogy as if you would die tomorrow. (I know that is a morbid thought, but it might get you on the right track.)

- What are the things that consume most of your time after work and sleep?

IMPORTANT SPACES

We spend many hours of our 24 hour day in our homes. How they are maintained has a tremendous impact on the quality of life for everyone living there. "We shape our dwellings and after that our dwellings shape us," is how Winston Churchill put it.

- Determine how you want a space to be used based on your priorities for it.

- Create a vision for what you want that space to look like. In observing unsuccessful attempts at being organized, I have determined that failing to decide what is really wanted or important for the space is the root of most of the problems I see. This is especially true when one is continually reorganizing a space.

- Take the time to think about every space you have and how you want to use it. The most important use of a space must be decided before any other actions take place. Sometimes the entire family may be involved in that decision if the space will be used by everyone, such as in the family room. But the needs in a bedroom or office may only require reflection and decisions by the person using that space.

- Items that will be put in that space and what should be removed are much easier decisions once the vision of each space is determined. Items you will need in the space can be kept or purchased and then arranged. Those items that will no longer be needed can be moved to more suitable spaces.

No matter how long it takes, coming to a decision about what is important in a space for the individual or the entire family will eventually be time well spent.

If this step is skipped, then the trials and errors of different scenarios for the space often result in frustration, dissatisfaction, possibly greater disorganization, and the accumulation of things that no longer have a use or function.

THE STUFF ISSUE IS A BIG ONE

A common problem in disorganization is too much stuff for the space. Let me say it another way. If you are disorganized it may be you have too many things in that space. We hate to admit it and we hate to let go of it, but too much can be a problem. In fact, it is the number one cause of disorganization that I see in my business.

More, More, More

We all have a deep seated emotional and spiritual need for more. Unfortunately we often try to fill the need for love, affection, worship, etc. with things rather than relationships that will meet those needs.

- You need to consider the role of your needs versus your wants as you plan for the spaces you want to organize.

- How much and how many are enough? Priorities require that you answer those questions for every area in your life, every space in your house and every activity in your schedule.

How much is enough clothes, enough gadgets, tools, appliances, enough toys, enough CDs, DVDs, fabric, beads, scrapbook paper or collectibles for you to have?

How frequently do you need to get the latest style of car, television, cell phone, home décor, or Vera Bradley purse? Do you keep and use things until they are worn out or no longer functional? If not, why not?

It is so easy to get caught up with gathering in more and more stuff. If one is good, then we think more is better. Our affluence has driven us and we have stuffed our homes.

The Need for Limits

If you cannot set limits on how much is enough, you will continue to accumulate things until there is no space left for them and you are back to making the decisions of what has top priority in your life and homes.

You need to evaluate each item you own and seriously consider your priorities and space before you make any new purchases.

Setting Limits

Decisions about limits can be made by deciding how much space you will give to items you own or how many items in a given category would be enough for you. If you collect classic movies on DVDs then ask yourself how many would be enough. Could you set a limit on what you would allow yourself to collect and would you have a space designated only for those movies that would contain them?

If a space is filled and you wanted to purchase another item in that category, then you have to decide if you can let another item go from that space. You can steal space from another reserved space there or elsewhere in the house and ruin your organizational system, or you can just stuff the new item in with the others and make it look messy. Lastly, you can simply decide to not make the purchase.

This same decision making process can be made with any items you own. Set limits for how much or how many you will allow in a space reserved for only that and then require any new items to answer those questions.

It might be a good idea to stop now and consider how you might set limits on the space you want to organize. These self-made boundaries give you new freedom in deciding on new purchases.

WHAT IS CLUTTER?

Clutter can be more than just the accumulations of things that didn't work in the space. It can be anything that we bought for the wrong reasons, that we no longer use or want, that has no home for placement, or that we are keeping for guilt or fear.

As a nation we have become driven to own the latest and greatest, to save everything and to allow things to be the number 1 priority in our expenditure of time, money, resources and relationships.

The following are some things that may be considered clutter. Look over the list and see if any apply to your situation.

Clutter—Things:

- That are out of place and you don't know what to do with them
- That you thought you would use but don't

- That you thought you wanted but don't
- That are broken or in disrepair
- That you know you have but can't find
- That belong to someone else
- That are out of date or expired
- That are duplicates
- That you don't know how to remove
- That you are keeping out of guilt
- That you are keeping for fear of needing them in the future. "But what if.......?"
- That you have no idea how you got them or why you have them

If any items come to your mind as you read that list, then stop and write those on a sheet of paper. In Chapter 7 we will discuss options for those things.

Clutter in Your Head

Clutter is not just a matter of stuff in your house but also clutter your head. Think about it. Not only has every thought you have ever had and every bit of knowledge you have ever learned been recorded in your brain, but also information on every item you have ever owned is there.

The decisions and processes of getting an item, using it, cleaning it, storing it, seeing it, touching it, etc. are all recorded in that gray matter. It stands to reason that the more things you have, the more cluttered you brain has become, especially in remembering where they are and why you have them.

I can't speak for you, but there are times that my brain's filing system has a hard time pulling up what I need in a timely manner. That delay might be from having to sort through the stuff that has accumulated through the years.

While we can't eliminate everything in our heads, we can eliminate the excess of things in our spaces and remove the need for the memories about them and then resist getting more things. Every little bit helps, right?

Clutter and Your Body

We could also add the effect clutter has on your body. Clutter and disorganization can cause stress that may raise your blood pressure and cause you to grind your teeth at night. It may also leave an unsafe environment allowing the opportunity for harm or injury to your body.

Linda, the perfectionist mentioned before, had a serious injury while we were removing items in a space that had not been unpacked. As she was carrying a large item out of the house, she caught her knuckle on the strike plate of a door jam along a cluttered hallway.

Our two hour visit to the emergency care center (you understand why she is so dear to me) revealed a serious cut. It was so deep that it could not be stitched but had to be braced and bandaged for several weeks so it could not be bent and reopen the wound. She also fell with that same object and bruised her knee. We laugh now about clutter being disastrous to your body, but I promised Linda I would tell her story in this book to emphasize how clutter can be hazardous to your health.

The Clutter Triangle

You can see how clutter can affect your body, mind and space, how each of those affects the others and causes you to be disorganized. It is wise to set yourself free from it once and forever. Let freedom ring.

Chapter 6

APPLYING THE
PRINCIPLES

We all want the spaces where we live and work to be attractive and efficient. Those with training in art and design and those with an eye for applying basic art principles use their talents and skills to make spaces attractive.

Professionals with organizational strategies, systems and tools use those to make the spaces functional and efficient. Often there is an overlapping of those roles.

The individual personality, preferences and processing style of the clients are the most important considerations in applying these principles to organizing. There are, however, some basic principles that are foundational to any organizational system.

The goal is to keep the systems simple since those that are too complex will be too difficult to maintain on a long term basis.

ZONES

After the decisions regarding the functions of spaces are made, those functions work best when the space is divided into zones or specific areas based on their use. A kitchen is often designed in that manner. The sink is the center of the cleaning zone, the range for the cooking zone, the pantry and refrigerator for the food storage zone.

Any space, large or small can be zoned in the same way. A bedroom can have a sleeping, dressing, reading or study zone. A large desk drawer can have a writing zone with pen, pencils, erasers, etc., a joining zone with paper clips, rubber bands, stapler, etc.; or a stationary zone with paper, envelopes, stamps, labels, etc.

Every zone needs a name to identify the space. A coat closet is a zone with a name as is the scrap booking shelf or the mail basket.

Some zones can be created by the furniture used for them such as the toy box and bins that are together in a room or by an area rug that joins several items together.

The zone principle is one of the first to be considered since it will determine:

- Which things are needed in the space
- How much room is needed for the things
- Where things are to be placed
- Any other considerations.

PLACING FOR CONVENIENCE

Some organizing principles are common sense to most of us. We have learned these from experience and use.

- Items should be placed where they are used.

- The more frequently items are used, the closer they should be. For example, dinnerware is best stored by the sink, dishwasher or serving area. Within that space the everyday dishes and flatware would be closer than those serving pieces used only on special occasions. Keep items near where you need them so putting them away is convenient.

- If space is limited, seasonal and special occasion items can be stored off site in another room or storage area since they are not used often.

- Duplicates of some items are needed for convenience. Things like pens, pencils and scissors are used in many different areas. Additional containers for these items should be placed where they are used.

Placing for Safety

- For safety reasons, heavier items should be stored in the lower sections of cabinets, closets, etc. Pulling down items that are too heavy or bulky from higher shelves can cause muscle strain or injury from falling objects that were too difficult to control.

- In filling containers choose smaller containers for heavy objects like books and linens since larger choices would be more difficult to lift and handle when full. The larger containers can be used for lighter items like baskets, pillows or Christmas wreaths.

- Not filling spaces to overflowing is another safety principle. When hallways are crowded or items are left in walkways and paths through the house, tripping and falling may cause serious injury.

The Permanent, Specific Home

Of all the principles given here, this is the most significant in placing and keeping order in the home.

- Every item you own needs a permanent, specific home. For example, not only might the shoes belong in the closet, but they should belong in the specific space in the shoe rack reserved for them. The hammer might not only belong in the garage, but it may belong in the top drawer of the tool box in the front divided section.

- There are no lost items if every item is returned to that home in a timely manner. This is one of the most difficult of the principles to apply because it requires a commitment to reserve a space for every item and return the item to it quickly. But it is the most rewarding because time is not lost looking for things and money is not lost buying duplicates of items that you cannot find.

- There are space limits for items. A basic organizing rule is to place only as many items in the space as it will reasonably and attractively hold. When items accumulate beyond the space reserved for them, then the decision of what to do with them becomes an organizational problem. I find this situation in many of my clients' homes because they try to put too many things in designated spaces. They continue to purchase more of those items but never get rid of any. Good organization requires setting limits which we have already discussed.

- There are identified and reserved spaces for every item and nothing else is allowed in that space. This principle keeps the spaces maintained, items can be found in less than a minute because you know where its home is located, and it constrains you in monitoring future purchases. You organize the spaces so they are functional and attractive and they can stay that way.

Use Containers Effectively

Items on shelves, in cabinets and even in drawers should be arranged so they do not fall on other items, move around in the space or mix with other items. Items should not remain in piles and should be easily found in a drawer rather than have to dig for them. One of the best ways to maintain good organization is by using containers.

In today's organizing happy world, there are containers available in every size, shape, color, material and price. There are even stores and outlets opened specifically for selling containers and organizing supplies. With so many choices, there should be something for everyone.

There are some guidelines to remember in choosing containers.

- Use the most attractive containers in places where they are on display or seen. Those containers used in closets, cabinets or drawers need not be as attractive or expensive.

- Keep like items together in containers. Do not mix types of items such as pens with paper clips or earrings with bracelets.

- If there is more than one of the same type of item, containerize them together.

- Separate items from each other in a drawer or cabinet with dividers or containers.

- Group small items on a shelf in containers. Sauce packets in a pantry and rings in a jewelry box are examples of items that could be grouped together.

- Containers should fit the space and hold the designated items in an orderly fashion.

- Measure spaces and items before purchasing any containers.

- Use square or rectangular containers whenever possible as they are more space efficient than round ones.
- Clear plastic containers are the most versatile and functional because you are able to see the contents clearly.

Decorative Containers

Fabric or paper covered containers and baskets are a great option for open shelves and tables. They are available in many sizes, styles and shapes and can be found in many price ranges. If baskets will be used for small items they should be tightly woven or lined with a material that will not allow items to fall through them.

Stacking Containers

Many containers are now designed to stack neatly on top of each other. These are good to use when several different types of items are stored on shelves. In one closet you may keep different types of seasonal items each in separate container that can be stacked.

If the items you stack are used often, stacking no more than two together is recommended. Digging out the bottom or middle container in a stack can be worrisome at best and hazardous if you are not very careful.

Plastic Stacking Drawers

A preferable option to stacking separate containers is to purchase stacking drawers. These come as small as a few inches square for beads, hair bows or spices to those over a foot wide and deep for socks, sweaters or linens.

Most units come with casters that can be snapped in allowing them to roll if put on the floor, or if you stay within the same style and brand, the top can be removed and another unit stacked upon it. In fact, within that same style you can separate the drawers themselves and reconfigure the stack making it one of the most versatile containers for organizing.

Functional Containers

Traditional plastic containers and plain cardboard are best for storing behind doors. They also come in an unlimited variety of styles and price ranges.

Some decorative containers are not functional so consider them carefully before purchasing them. Toothbrush holders are one example of this. While one may be very functional and look nice on the counter, if it is one that has a limited number of holes for the brushes, it may be inadequate for your situation. The opposite might also be true. Spice racks that have more container spaces than you use or need are not an efficient use of space.

The following chapter has more information about making purchases including containers and other organizing products.

Trays as Containers

An attractive way to hold some items on counters, tables, tops of dressers and chests, coffee tables, etc. is with trays. These come in a variety of sizes, shapes and materials. They can contain small items that may otherwise be scattered around those areas.

Use Labels

Labels should be used on any container that does not have one. In addition, labels should be put on both ends of containers that are removed often so that after returning them the label is always seen.

Many self-adhesive labels come in various sizes, colors and shapes and can be found in office supply stores or any place that carries stationery items.

Some of these are available in sheets that can be used with computer printers and the instructions for using them are included.

The electronic label maker is the organizer's best friend. It produces labels that are easy to read and give uniformity to the containers that have them. Use them on file folders, the fronts of containers, the edges of shelves and more.

Some labels are especially helpful in newly organized spaces where items in containers cannot be seen.

Temporary Labels

Some other types of labels can be used temporarily until one becomes familiar with the location of items.

A couple of years ago I planned and executed the organization of a kitchen in a new spacious home. It had been so poorly designed by the builder that we had to completely rearrange the placement of the pantry items and the dinnerware used by the family to make it more functional.

After the items in the cabinets were switched and organized, I placed sticky notes on the cabinet doors and printed labels on the edges of the shelves inside. This allowed the family to find what they needed and return items to their permanent home until they had memorized their new locations.

Some areas and containers may never need labels, but when in doubt, it is a good option.

USE HIDDEN SPACES

Being content where you live and being organized in a space you think is too small can be a challenge. You might think a 3000 square foot house would be easier to organize than a 1000 square foot house. The challenges may be different, but the principles are the same. If your space seems just too small for the things you need, then using hidden spaces is one way to stretch the storage or display space you already have in your home.

Under the Bed

Many organizers do not support the use of under the bed storage, but I consider it one of those great hidden spaces in smaller homes. (I do not advocate throwing dirty clothes under them as my children did when required to clean their rooms.) This space is ideal for storing off season clothing and other items that are not needed frequently.

Currently there are many types of containers designed specifically for under the bed storage and it is a good choice to use them. Most are wide, flat and covered and are usually made of fabric or plastic.

If your bed is too close to the floor for storage, bed lifts can be purchased to raise it up.

Behind Closed Doors

Another hidden space is behind entry doors to rooms. Most doors are placed in the corners of walls, but the door frame itself provides a narrow storage area when the door is open and a very accessible space when the door is closed.

Racks can be placed on the wall itself or on the back of the door to hang many types of items. If you do not want to attach anything directly to the door, there are over the door style racks or hooks for nearly every type item that needs organizing.

Some racks can be used for more than one type of item as the storage spaces on them are versatile. Clothing, hats, scarves, necklaces or neckties, are just a few of the items that can be placed there.

These racks can also be put on the inside of swinging closet doors for more storage options.

Up and on Top

For those that have collectible items that are for display only, placing shelving above windows is an option to expand display areas. Shelves over doors can also be used for unbreakable items that might fall if the door is slammed.

Space on the tops of kitchen and bathroom cabinets that do not reach the ceiling can also be used for display of rarely used items. These spaces are ideal because they are so high that they do not need to be cleaned often unless there is a problem with allergies in the home. They can provide space for items that are special to the owner but impractical to keep close at hand. Decorative plates, family photographs and collectible books are examples of things that work well on higher shelves.

The tops of tall pieces of furniture such as bookcases, wardrobes and chests would be useful for the same types of items.

Hidden Spaces in Cabinets and Closets

- Some cabinets and bookcases have adjustable shelves. To reduce the wasted space above items, you can lower the shelf above and add additional shelves in the new space provided.
- Wire shelf racks and two tiered turntables are options for adding space between shelves by creating additional levels of storage within the space. Corner units are available to make the most of those spaces too.
- Don't forget about using the space above the top shelf in closets. Additional shelves can often be added above those to expand storage

possibilities. If the hanging rod is lowered in a closet, more shelves can be added above it. This may be especially convenient in a child's room.

- Narrow shelving can also be placed on walls where furniture is difficult to arrange such as between close windows or in hallways or entry areas.

Staircases

If you have staircases in your home there is often space hidden under the stairs that is great for storing off-season items. These spaces can be creatively organized with shelves, hooks or racks so that things are not just bagged up and thrown in them. That is an easy temptation since it is out of sight. Be creative with that space and make it organized too.

Multi-Purpose Furniture

Functional pieces of furniture can offer additional storage space when needed. Window seats and ottomans with storage under the cushions are a good choice. And purchased furniture that has storage built in it such as coffee tables, end tables and night stands can be great for organizing. Choose those with drawers or cabinet doors when possible so they can function without having to clean them as often as open shelving.

Adding fabric skirts to sofas and chairs or hanging linens to the floor over tables provides hidden space for storage. Board games, videos and CDs are some of the items that can be kept there.

Some furniture can serve more than one purpose when moved to another room. Chests can hold linens when moved to a dining room, desks can be used as vanity dressers in a bedroom, china cabinets can become bookcases, etc. Let your creativity come forth as you organize.

Up the Walls

When square footage is limited in a home, you can consider using all available vertical wall space for adding display or storage shelves, cabinets, hooks, etc. With ceilings at 8' or 9' and even higher in some homes, there is plenty of room for expanding upwards.

Walls are a great place to express your creativity, too. Rather than add clutter to table tops with figurines, candles, etc., decorate you walls with paintings, portraits or needlework to add charm and personality to your spaces.

Light the Way

Lighting makes a room appear larger and more spacious. For spaces to be used safely and effectively, adequate light is needed. When you are organizing have plenty of light available and plan for good lighting in the space when you are done.

Natural light is best, but when it is not available or in the evening, sufficient artificial light should be provided. Lamps, stick on globes or built in canisters can be used to add needed light.

Overhead lights are good for multipurpose uses, but additional lighting may be needed under counters, over sinks, in closets and in other storage areas. Some projects and tasks require a light source of their own.

Not only will good lighting make your space brighter, but it will show off your organizing efforts.

Chapter 7

WHAT IS IN OUR SPACES AND SCHEDULES?

ow that you have the overall principles and strategies, how do you get started? Start small. The best advice I can give is to limit the size of your first organizing project. Begin with a drawer, closet, bookcase, etc. Success in small areas will boost your confidence and motivate you to continue with the process in larger spaces.

Another recommendation is to start with an area that is the most irritating to you or is the most visible. It is not a good idea to take on an entire room as your first project.

Spaces do not become disorganized over night, and one session will not provide enough time to get them organized. Be patient and take it one step at a time. Planning ahead will make the process much smoother.

Take Pictures

I recommend that you take pictures of the space before you begin. Not only will you see the area in a more objective light, but you will have the great before and after pictures that everyone loves to see. Take one shot from a distance and then get a few close-up views so that you don't miss any details.

While I am on this subject, you should have pictures of all the spaces in your house for insurance purposes. Some organizers suggest that you open every closet, drawer and cabinet so that nothing is overlooked.

Rather than pictures, you may want to take videos with your own commentary about the things that are in each space. This makes a great inventory of your things if ever needed, and it will open you eyes about how things really appear.

Be sure to include the garage, attic and outside to record the outdoor items and landscaping you have. (I did this before and after hurricane Isabel blew over trees in my yard and on my house. We were told by the insurance company we could have the roof fixed immediately and they would reimburse us. Weeks later their adjustor looked at our before and after pictures of the damaged areas and gave us full credit for the repairs and losses.)

Keep a Notebook

It is a good organizational strategy to keep a record of where you want to go and how to get there with any project. Even for organizing a drawer you can take notes to describe the process and when you might want to do it. Some small jobs can be organized while you are using them.

For larger projects you might want to include the following.

- Your vision for the space. Include your goals for the space, its uses and what you want to see in it. This is very important because it will give the most satisfaction over a longer period of time and will keep you from reorganizing the space over and over again.

- Clippings you have taken from magazines, sketches of ideas you have and the before picture.
- A list of organizing items with their costs
- Any tools and supplies you may need
- Your proposed budget
- A schedule.

Having these things written in one place makes it much easier to stay on task and get the job done.

TOOLS, SUPPLIES AND MORE

Once you have decided what you want for the space and have some ideas of what will be needed there, make a list of the tools you will need to do the work. This may be as simple as cleaning supplies for a drawer or as complicated as hardware tools for a closet redo.

Sorting Containers

Even small projects need sorting bins, boxes or other containers to hold items as they are removed from the project space. Depending on the size of the space, a few gallon or quart size containers would be good. For larger spaces, laundry baskets, dish pans or cardboard boxes are better choices. In some spaces you may need both. Try to anticipate what your needs will be.

Cleaning Supplies

It is a good idea to have cleaning gloves, dust cloths, and a vacuum nearby whatever the project. Use black trash bags for trash and clear bags for recycling or donations in order to keep the sorting easier.

Repair Tools

A repair kit and paint may be needed in some spaces. Depending on the project, a few simple tools or painting supplies may be needed. If there is major damage or if an extensive remodel or redesign is planned, expert help many be necessary.

Organizing Supplies

Organizing supplies, containers, bins, racks, etc. may be needed to make the project successful and you should plan for which would work best in each space. Before making any purchases, be sure to measure the space carefully and record it in your notebook. Be sure your purchases will fit and keep any receipts until you are sure it does the job you expected. It is a good idea to also measure the items that will go into any containers since that is as important as the space it will fill.

Specialty items for organizing can be very useful if they fit the space and hold the necessary items. Do not be swayed by the most attractive or expensive gadgets unless they will fit your needs.

Many containers can have multiple uses if you think outside the box. Over the door shoe bags can hold socks, mittens, jewelry, gardening tools, sewing notions, toys and more. Tall kitchen trash cans make great storage for rolls of wrapping paper, and dishpans can hold file folders. The goal is to give a permanent specific home to your things.

Dividers

There are many organizing items now available that will and divide areas in drawers, double or triple levels within your shelves and separate items stacked on them. Most discount stores now have a variety of organizing supplies so you can be sure to get what fits your space and satisfies your needs.

It may help for you to search online or check out several stores before making your purchases. You will be able to see what items are available and the comparative features and costs before committing to them.

Recycled Organizers

One smart move is to consider using items you already have on hand and give them a new purpose. This is a good way to make recycling a part of your project. Everyday household items can be given a new life. I am not an advocate of saving every margarine container or Pringles can, but a few could be given a new life in a new home.

Cereal boxes can hold magazines or thinner how to books, egg crates will divide children's hair bows and jewelry or beads, cans can be covered as pencil or art brush holders; and stationery boxes can be reused to contain notepads, stamps and labels. Pill containers can hold beads, pizza boxes are perfect for scrapbook papers, and mismatched mugs can hold flowers or plants.

The possibilities are endless but I will restate the obvious. Don't save every container just in case you might be able to use it in the future. This includes saving it with the noble thought that you might use it to be organized. Unless you have an immediate use for the item let it go and be free of it.

BUDGETS

Part of the planning process is to consider the finances that will be needed to complete the project. It may be a few dollars for a drawer divider or considerably more for a closet redesign or a room make over complete with new furniture. Include the following items in your proposal.

- A set amount of funds allowed for the project. Planning your purchases ahead of time will help you stay within that amount.

- A list of the things you need and stick to it when you shop. Unplanned projects have a way of going over budget and leaving one with residual negative feelings about trying another organizing adventure.

- A list of items you may want to sell. Funds from the items you remove and no longer need may help recoup the expenses of getting new items for the space. If you can sell some of the things before beginning the project, it may make it easier to keep the budget on target.

- A record of all expenses in your notebook so you can adjust your spending if necessary. It is better to maintain the amounts as you go so there are no unpleasant surprises before you complete the project.

SCHEDULES

Putting your project on a specific date on the calendar is the best way to get it done. You may need to adjust it, but putting it there will serve as a reminder.

- For smaller jobs only a few hours may be needed but it should be given a specific date and time. Timing the organizing session before the weekend may provide items for a Saturday yard sale.

- Larger projects can be given a suggested completion date and add back dates for portions of the work to be completed. Allow sufficient time but do not postpone getting it done.

- Flexibility is a virtue but staying with the planned schedule is the preferred method of finishing on time. If hired contractors (not professional organizers) are used in your projects, you may have to throw all schedules to the wind and pray there will eventually be a completion of it. (Again I speak from experience.)

CONSIDER ASSISTANCE

Small organizing jobs can be completed without help. On larger projects, organizing can be even more fun when you share it with someone. (I am not joking.) You do need to be careful who gets pulled into the job since the success of it will depend on your relationship and the objectivity of those involved.

When organizing your own things or spaces used mainly by you, anyone you like or enjoy working with is fine. When organizing things that belong to others, they should be involved in the process. Otherwise you may find yourself making company with the family canine.

• Project Groups

One suggestion for assistance is used by a client that belongs to a "project group" of four friends. They give themselves a cute name for identity and one day each week three of them show up at the fourth person's house to work on a project.

They might paint a bathroom, bake cookies for the church bake sale, plant flowers or scrub the deck. Whatever is needed that week is planned by and for the host member. Each week a different member is host so each person is visited once a month. Lots of good things get done and so far there have been no law suits.

This type of group is perfect for organizing projects. Once they have learned the principles and process at the first few sessions, they are like professionals and can move from room to room and house to house with expertise. (My guess is they would be a great motivational asset.)

- ## Other Assistance

    Perhaps you have a good friend or relative that will barter a day of organizing for a day of babysitting or some other task. Be sure this person will not be judgmental about your situation and will be helpful in supporting your decisions as you work. Being able to keep your affairs confidential is as important as the strength of their legs and back.

    Your spouse may or may not be a good choice depending on your initial choice of a spouse. (I will let that rest and move on.)

    Of course I will gladly recommend a professional organizer if you think that is the best choice. One client called me after seeing a feature article about my business in the local newspaper. Her initial comment was, "If you are sick you need a doctor and if you are disorganized you need an organizer." We got to work right away and helped her make great changes in her spaces. Hopefully this book will give you the information to move forward without our help but I will discuss our assistance in Chapter 10.

GET READY FOR O-DAY

If you have planned the organizing event, you have your notebook filled with information, the date is set on the calendar, you have purchased the necessary items and you have enlisted help if you need it.

- ## Remove Interruptions

    It is a good idea to plan for babysitting if needed and you should notify those close to you that you will be unable to take phone calls, answer text messages or e-mails during that time. As much as possible you want to eliminate any interruptions. Do not allow yourself to get distracted by other needs you see as you work.

- ## Food and Drink

  If it will be an all day affair, plan a lunch break ahead of time so it will not take more than 30 minutes. Keep water on hand so staying hydrated will not impede the flow of adrenalin as you work.

- ## Dress for Success

  Have comfortable clothing for the project and shoes with good support and non slip soles for safety. Injury is a painful excuse for getting sidetracked. (No pun intended)

- ## Audio, not Video

  If you are addicted to certain television programs and those will be airing during your project, make arrangements to have them saved. (We will discuss its effect on time management in Section IV) This will not be a good time to be glued to the boob tube.

  You should plan for some peppy music to enhance your success. If a local radio station is dependable you may use it or load in one of your CDs or tapes to provide continuous stimulation. Forget the waltzes, blues, hymns, sentimental songs or classical dirges. You may want John Phillips Souza, some happy 1960s doo-wap but not hysterical hard metal to keep you bouncing along. I think you get the idea.

What Happened to the Best Made Plans?

Life happens and your good plans may get off schedule. Physical illness of those involved, tragic events and other situations may come up that can interrupt your plans.

And it is not a good idea to organize when you are emotionally upset or angry. You may make decisions that you will regret later on. You should postpone the organizing until you and your situation are back to normal.

Flexibility is as valuable a trait as well as being organized. Hopefully you will eventually have both.

Chapter 8

USING THE
ORGANIZING PROCESS

When the organizing time arrives you need to get your brain in gear. We are all distracted by many things from the time we get up until we go to bed. As you approach the organizing project, you want to get rid of as many distractions as possible.

Read over the entries in your notebook. This will help you focus on the task at hand and program your thinking about what you want to do. If you have assistance, it is a good idea to go over the details of the project with them.

Keep a can-do attitude throughout the process. Organizing is a learned skill that is worth the effort. Like driving a car for the first time, it may seem scary or difficult, but the more you do it the better you will be at it. Try to enjoy each step of the process and finish one space before going on to another.

Use some positive self talk to remind yourself of how much you will love the new space. There will be some hard decisions to make as you work. Try to enjoy the process, keep a sense of humor and stay focused.

Break old routines or habits. Be committed to the process and ready for lifestyle changes when you are finished. You will begin to see results in each step you take. Success will bring freedom that will make it worth all the hard work.

Now, get all of your supplies together, turn on the music and pray, I mean proceed.

THE 3 Ps

The organizing process can be divided into three basic steps. They are:

Purge—removing the items in the space

Pitch—getting items that do not belong there out of the area

Place—finding a specific permanent home for what you are keeping

PURGE

As you begin organizing, clear as much as possible from the space, one area at a time. Do not remove large furniture unless those pieces will be eliminated permanently from the room. Clean out one drawer at a time, one closet at a time, etc. If there is not enough space to completely purge it, move what is left out of the way.

The Sorting Process

As you purge, sort what you are moving. I normally put the black trash bag, the clear recycle bag and donation bags in laundry baskets for support.

Since laundry baskets may actually contain laundry at the time, purchase several of them and some dishpans from the local dollar or discount stores to use just for sorting. These can also be used for sorting items that do not belong in that space as well as separating the categories of items that will remain.

It is not unusual to use 6-10 laundry baskets for a room or over a dozen dishpans for an office or drawers.

Sorting as you purge eliminates having a separate step of sorting after purging. The more sorting you do now will make placement later on an easier process. Label each container with its contents or destination. You can begin sorting in these general categories:

- Trash
- Recycling
- Keep
- For Sale
- Donate
- Off Site or belongs elsewhere

For the most success, touch each item only once and answer these questions.

QUESTIONS TO ASK AS YOU SORT

You must answer the question of why you have each item *if* you keep it.

- You saved it because you thought it would be useful. Have you used it? If not, would you go out and buy one today? If not, remove it.
- Have you used it in the last year? If not, move it on.
- Why did you buy it? Media pressure, keeping in style, impulse purchase, on sale? If it is not needed or in use, move it on.
- Could I borrow, rent or improvise if I need it? If so, remove it.
- Would it be too expensive or difficult to replace? If so and you like it, keep it.
- Is it out of date, out of style, expired, broken, torn, or no longer useful? If so, remove it.
- Is it more trouble to maintain than pass on? If so, move it on.

- Do I love or value it? If keeping it for sentimental reasons take a picture and pass it on to another caring person who wants or needs it and has room for it. If you love it enough to maintain it and make space for it, consider keeping it. Do not hide it in a box in storage. That dishonors it.

- Is guilt making you keep it? Free yourself and it. You will feel ten times lighter.

- Would you move it to a smaller house? If not, why keep it now?

- Do you want to leave it for your children to have or handle? See if they want it or will take it now. You will be surprised by what they do not like or want.

- Am I keeping it because of the fear of "what if I may need it after it is gone"? If so, acknowledge it will be available to purchase later on should you actually need it.

- Does it make life better for me? If not, why keep it?

- If it doesn't belong in this space, where will it be kept permanently? If you cannot answer that, move it on.

Sorting Trash/Recycling

Many items from the space will need to be removed permanently. When I speak of putting them in the trash, I realize different localities require different methods, schedules and containers for disposing of different types of items. Please respect those requirements and sort your disposed items accordingly.

This is where you leave your ego at the altar. Undoubtedly you will uncover things you did not realize were there as you purge. Your son's booger collection may appear in your lingerie drawer or you daughter's lollipop wrappers in your kitchen cabinets. You get the idea. Those items are obviously trash and should go directly in the bag without comment as fast as possible.

Other trash is not so obvious.

- Clothing that is in disrepair beyond recovery as well as what you are not willing to have repaired should be trashed. If it is not nice enough to give to your family or friends, it is not good enough to donate.

- Do not donate such items to charity thrift shops or save for a yard sale. Who wants to take on your problems? I know it sounds heartless, but thrift shop workers will tell you they will do the same thing.

- The same question goes for clothing that is worn out. Unless it is a pair of jeans that can be cut off, no one wants threadbare clothing. Put yourself in their shoes and be considerate.

- Expired products, obsolete appliances and broken electronics should also be trashed. The old 45 and 78 rpm records are not even wanted by the stores that sell those oldies but goodies. (Trust me; I have been to them with my father's collection.) As heart wrenching as it is, put them in the appropriate bag to be disposed permanently. Trying to sell them may prove more trouble than they are worth.

- Do not save items for parts. No matter where they go, do not save items for the good parts they still have. My mother would cut buttons off clothing and my dad saved screws, bolts and nails from items no longer usable. Those parts were never used again, and it is very doubtful you would use what you save.

It is not uncommon to have several bags of trash/recycling/disposables filled when organizing a room or closet. Close them and take them out as soon as possible. Out of sight and out of mind allows freedom to flood in.

Sorting Items to Keep

All is not lost. The good thing is that you will keep some of the things in the space. These need to be sorted by categories.

- Label a separate container for each category. For large spaces this may take many containers but it makes replacing the items in an organized manner much easier.

- For hanging items in a closet, I usually stack those in separate piles on the bed. If that space is not convenient, they can be categorized on the closet rod as you purge. That does not work if the closet needs repair, reconfiguring or painting.

- If the items belong in another room (the clothes brush in your kitchen utensil drawer) label a container for that room and place those items in it.

- Items you are keeping but need cleaning or repairing should be separated from the others. Put soiled clothing in the laundry and anything that needs to be professionally cleaned in the car. This will prevent procrastination which may result in returning them to the closet.

- Items that need repair should be placed in the car also unless you can repair them yourself. If it is not done within a month, let them go to the trash.

- Borrowed items should be labeled and returned as soon as possible in good condition with a note of thanks (and possibly apology).

Sorting Items for Sale

The "but I spent good money for it" problem for saving items can often be solved by selling them. This can be a good thing or a disappointing heartbreak.

Some items you have are in good condition and may be useful to someone else. There is certainly nothing wrong with advertising large items for sale or having a yard sale when you have sufficient items to do so. Of course you are advertising to the world that you have been the victim of collecting too much stuff.

Consignment shops are very successful in some areas so you might want to look into that possibility. Another option is eBay. If you are already a seller, this may be an easy project for you. Craig's List and other online sources as well as the local classifieds can be considered if you have the time to pursue those choices.

To be successful in your organizing projects, you must be willing to permanently let go of any items that do not sell.

Sorting the Valuables

I am sure you have seen the exhilaration of the Antiques Roadshow guests upon learning their grandmother's vase, necklace or side chair is worth thousands of dollars. It would follow in your hopeful imagination that surely your collections, inheritances or great finds would do the same. I hate to be the spoiler here, but it is not likely. If in doubt, there are appraisers in every town who can answer that question for you.

At this point you need to decide if these items are important to you personally. Do you use it or display it? Is it packed away in a box in storage somewhere only to be seen again when your estate is settled?

If it is really worth something to you, it must be treated as such and boxing it up is not the way to do that. Allowing it to be stored out of site diminishes its value.

No ancestor would be pleased with that and neither should you. It is better to move it on to someone who will give it the dignity and respect it deserves. You will be demonstrating its value by moving it on.

Sorting Sentimental Items to Pass On

Family members are a great start when you consider letting go of items that have a sentimental or monetary value. It is a good idea to see if any of them are interested and would enjoy having the things. It would be up to them to carry the responsibility of ownership.

There may be set of china that was handed down through your family and you have never used it. See if there is someone else in the family that could use it, display it or enjoy having it. You can rest in the fact that it is in good hands and enjoy the freedom from that responsibility.

Sorting Practical Items to Donate

Some items are no longer useful to you but may be to someone else. Baby clothes that are outgrown may be needed by a family you know expecting their first child. You may have updated your décor and no longer need the original draperies, bedspreads or chair cushions. You should never feel guilty about donating anything. It is a charitable thing to do.

One local shop owner raised money for the American Cancer Society's Relay for Life by asking for donations of hats and purses from her customers to be sold to raise money for the cause. She confessed she had personally hoarded many purses but was relieved when they were purchased by someone who wanted them more than she did. Not only were the items being purchased by someone who would enjoy them, but funds were raised to help a very worthy cause.

If you do not know anyone personally that could use or enjoy your items then donating them to local charities is an excellent way to put them to good use. Many people are worried that letting go of the things takes away from their value. The opposite is true when they are passed on to someone who needs them. Allowing items to be stashed away in a closet is certainly not acknowledging their value.

A young mother in our church told of how she managed to keep her children clothed and with toys when their income was reduced for an extended period of time. Several times she went to thrift stores to find clothing and other items at prices she could afford. Those who had donated had blessed her by providing what she needed.

Be encouraged that making donations of things you no longer need, use or enjoy may be ways you can "pay forward" a blessing to someone you do not know.

Donating Tax Deductible Items

It is becoming increasingly important to keep good records on items you donate to charities and other non-profit organizations. On a separate sheet of paper make five columns to record: the **date** of the donation, the **description** of each item (Arrow shirt), the **original cost** to the best of your knowledge, **quantity** of those items and the amount the charities consider the fair market resale **donation value**. Taking pictures is a good idea, too.

All of this should be stapled to the receipt that the charity gives you. In your tax records file include a copy of the charities' donation guides as documentation for your claims.

One lady at my speaking engagement to a garden club told how she was audited by the IRS but they never questioned her charitable deductions because she had the records I described to you.

The resource section has the contact information for the donation value of items.

"I Am Not Sure" Items

In every organizing session there are always some items that fall into the category of not knowing what to do with them. Decisions cannot be made at the moment to keep it or let it go. This might be a good place to ask for help in deciding what to do. "In the midst of council there is safety."

As a last resort, you may box it up, label the box and date it. If an item is needed in the future, it can be found easily. Remember, it will take up valuable space in you house.

If it is not opened in 6 months or a year at most, then it can be sent off to a charity unopened, and I repeat, unopened.

PITCH

This part of the process often takes place simultaneously with the sorting and purging. It requires that you remove any items that will no longer be used in that space.

- Items that belong in another room can be moved immediately.
- Items that need to be permanently disposed can be moved out when the bag is full.
- Set a deadline for items to be removed that will be passed on to others. Individuals that will receive the items need to know when you expect the things to be picked up or you should arrange a time to deliver them. Large items that might go to someone out of town may need to be stored for a time, but there should be a deadline for it.
- Arrange for some charities to pick up items on their regular pick up schedule or ask for a specific date if they can accommodate it.
- Items that need to be cleaned or repaired can go to the car at the end of the organizing session. They should be dropped off at the next trip or as soon as possible.
- The "I am not sure items" should be immediately boxed and removed as stated above.
- Check to be sure that only the things that will be kept are remaining in the space.

Additional items hanging around will only tempt you to find a place for them. They will be robbing you of your square footage.

The Remodeling Strategy

There is another strategy that can be used in preparing a space to be reorganized. Often when large remodeling projects take place, all items in the space are boxed up and labeled until the project is completed. At that time the items are unpacked and placed in their new spaces.

For those who need a more drastic approach to their organizing process the same strategy can be used. When the space is cleaned out, everything is put in boxes and labeled. Then nothing is removed from a box until it is actually needed. At that point it can be given a permanent home in the space. After 6 months those items still remaining in the boxes have obviously not been used. These are donated.

Not Your Things?

As you purge and pitch items, another golden rule of things is never dispose of any items that do not belong to you. It is a good idea to separate those things into separate containers for the owner to sort. An older woman in one of my workshops told of bagging up dated golfing magazines that her husband had kept for years.

She put the bag in a container under a staircase and when she found it several years later in an organizing session she showed it to him. He had to admit he had never missed them and allowed her to get rid of them. This stalling method might work for those hesitant to let things go, but never dispose of them permanently without their permission.

PLACE

This is the most rewarding part of the organizing process. The things that have been kept will be organized and placed in a specific permanent home reserved for them. Be sure the space is clean and repaired if necessary.

The placement of the items should follow the guidelines discussed in the section on organizing principles in Chapter 6. This will facilitate the success of the newly organized spaces. Sometime a sketch or drawing of how you want the space to look will help as you return the items. Remember you want the space to be functional and attractive.

Using the Supplies

If you have purchased organizing supplies to make the space more efficient, now is the time to try them out. Dividers for drawers are an excellent way to keep items in place and racks, containers and dividers are great for cabinets and shelves.

Any products that are not a good fit should be returned for exchange or refund. Do not keep them just in case you might need them later on. They will be available if such a need arises.

This may be a process of trial and error placement. Configuring small spaces are usually more difficult than larger ones. Two heads are better than one if you get stuck as you organize and is another reason to consider assistance.

The Specific Permanent Home—Again

One day when I was away from home, my married daughter was visiting my husband and called to ask where she could find a receipt. It was for a guaranteed plant we had purchased several months earlier but had died. In less than a minute I directed her to the particular file cabinet, drawer and file that held the receipt. It had a specific permanent home that was immediately accessible.

This is not an uncommon scenario when you use good organizing principles. Of all the principles I teach my clients, this is the one they say has made the biggest difference in their lives. Getting to this point is a worthwhile goal and has great rewards.

It may take a little while to get used to where things are and labels may be needed temporarily. But when the system is a fit, you will never have to worry about where things belong and you will know exactly where to go when you need them. It is a basic organizing principle and it gives the greatest feeling of freedom.

Leave Empty Spaces

It is not a good idea to organize each space until it is completely filled or packed to capacity. It is a good idea to leave empty spaces in every project. This allows for important future purchases and for replacement items that may be larger than the original.

The rubber spatula you have now may get damaged and a good replacement is larger. And how many of us have replaced our old cassette tapes with CDs that are larger? It is also more visually appealing to have vacant spaces. Open spaces appear larger and more organized.

Prepare for Changes

Flexibility may be needed after the organizing system is put in place. If the system is just not working for you, then try another arrangement that may be better. There is nothing wrong with changing things around.

Peggy is a lawyer that has an office in her home. Her desire was to create an attractive box there to sort her mail and incoming papers. We set up some labeled hanging folders in a beautifully papered box to take care of them, but after a few weeks we realized that was not a good placement for it.

As she came in the house after work, she would immediately set the papers down on the nearby surface so she could take her dog outside. Most often she would not get around to sorting the papers in her office until there was a considerable pile. Placing the sorting box closer to the door rather than in her office was a better arrangement for her in keeping her papers organized.

Chapter 9

FINDING PLACES FOR HELP

if you are completely overwhelmed at this point and are fearful that this organizing thing is too much for you, you are not alone. Some tasks appear to be more than we can handle. This is especially true if you have put off organizing for a long time or if there are many spaces that need help.

TELEVISION MIRACLES

Be encouraged that Rome wasn't built in a day and most organizing projects are not completed as quickly as it seems on television. Programs such as *Clean Sweep* and *Mission Organization* can create the illusion that room makeovers are completed in 30 or 60 minute time slots.

Think about it. Each program has a team of assistants that design, remodel, make purchases and create the new spaces from beginning to end. Each one of those segments takes a team about 80 hours of actual on the job productivity. Don't we wish we had that kind of assistance?

Books

It is evident now that you like to read and there are many other books besides this one that can help you as you consider organizing your spaces. Some have a definite focus on one particular area such as garages, kitchens or children's rooms. They may give you some new ideas for your spaces that will make the organizing process much easier.

Other organizing books discuss in more detail the emotional and mental problems associated with disorganization. These are especially helpful for those who are friends or relatives of hoarders or those chronically disorganized.

Websites

The world of electronics, telecommunications and other technologies has not been neglected by professional organizers and those related industries. Any web search will bring up thousands of sites that have useful organizing information. Most professional organizers have their own business site as well as blogs and other Internet activities.

Privacy to get more information for solving specific organizational problems and convenience are some of the reasons these sites are appealing. Some sites allow downloading information and others provide an exchange of ideas for problem solving.

Professional Organizers

The most effective way to get help with organizing is to contact a professional organizer. Many of them, including myself, belong to the National Association of Professional Organizers which provides ethical standards and continuing education for its members.

While it is the prominent organization for our profession, there are other related organizations including the National Study Group on Chronic Disorganization and Faithful Organizers. I also belong to both of those and can recommend their organizers as upholding high standards of competence and proficiency. You can also find organizers in your area through the Find My Organizer web site.

• Competence

Professional organizers are competent in assessing the situation and making action plans to create orderly places. We have learned the principles and systems that are basic to all organizing and how to interpret them to individual situations. We are familiar with effective products for organizing and can recommend other resources for help.

We not only assist our clients but we educate them so that organizing skills are transferred to them. This allows for their continued success in organizing.

• Creative

With solid organizing principles in mind, we are often able to find a new functions for items you may already have and new arrangements for better use of spaces. We are able to find appropriate strategies that match each individual and their organizing style.

• Compassionate and Caring

Just like nurses are trained to treat injuries in the emergency room without being overcome by blood, gunshots, broken bones, etc., professional organizers are trained to treat mounds of papers, bags of trash and lots of clutter without judgment or criticism. We are compassionate and caring individuals who are compelled to help our clients.

We know the person is not their stuff, and we get satisfaction in seeing our clients enjoy their organized spaces and continue maintaining them. We keep contact over a period of time for assistance if needed and often become friends.

• Cost Effective

Although we charge for our services, we are cost effective. Before beginning any assessment or project we will give you an estimate of the costs so that you can make an informed decision about choosing to use our help.

Erin hired me to help organize her walk-in closet. She had considered hiring another company that wanted to completely redesign the space and install new furnishings in it. That estimate was considerably more than what I charged her. Not only did I save her money but also time since we were able to complete the project in one morning the week she called.

Helping you prevent lost time and items in the future is part of the value we provide. "Solutions for saving time, space and resources" was chosen as the byline for my company because my vision is to provide those things.

• Confidential

Finally professional organizers are confidential. We are absolute in keeping the identities of our clients private. Although we often take pictures, they never include names. No one including my husband is given the names of my clients. (For security reasons he is given the address of a new client and we have a plan for checking to be sure I am safe after I arrive at the appointment for the first time.)

Although many clients are relieved at the confidentiality clause in my contracts, all have volunteered to have their names used as a referral after the job is done.

A listing of some of my favorite books, websites and organizations for more help has been included in the resource section. These may give you more information in your organizing journey.

Chapter 10

KEEPING IT ORGANIZED

Once you have finished your organizing project you must make a commitment to keep it that way. You can no longer maintain the habits you had before or the space will become disorganized once again. Like all lifestyle changes, it must come from the inside out, be an everyday commitment and not a one shot event.

GOOD HABITS

Learning a new system will take time and deliberate choices. Returning items to their permanent homes is imperative in keeping the system maintained. This may require breaking old habits and establishing new ones.

I have heard it takes 21 days to do this but I have observed it is much easier to build new habits in organizing. The immediate visual change in the space after the project is completed is a strong motivator to keep it that way. While it will take a change in the way things have been handled in the past, having an observable result for a new system is worth taking the time and effort to maintain it.

FLEXIBILITY

Most organizing projects and systems are very successful without any changes but some will require adjustments after they are used for a few weeks. Making those changes is as important as beginning the organizing process.

If it becomes obvious that adjusting to the new system is working against your personality, skills or general sanity then some changes need to be made. Often it is a simple relocating of items that are used frequently or removal of things that are hindering the system. Be flexible, make a few adjustments and try again. Realize that it took a long time for things to get disorganized and it may take time to make the system a good fit for you.

WATCH THE PUT DOWN

Part of making the system effective is what you decide about the things in your hands. Avoiding the temptation to put things down temporarily or indiscriminately is a good first step. If these items you are holding must be taken to rooms in the other parts of the house, then relocating containers are a good idea.

These containers are usually baskets, fabric covered boxes or similar attractive items. They can be placed at the top or bottom of staircases and at entry/exit doors. You must remember to clear them out at the earliest convenience so the items are returned in a timely manner. This means they are emptied at least once a day. Keep those containers empty before you go to bed.

Controlling Incoming Items

After spaces are organized train yourself to love clean surfaces and empty spaces so much that you will hate to destroy it. Overfilling those spaces can do just that.

More stuff means more maintenance, time to clean, store, etc. Less really is more—more peace and more freedom.

• One In, One Out

Before any new items come into the space there are some organizing decisions that must be made. The one in, one out system is a great process for keeping the space organized. If you want a new gadget, then one you already own must go. Realizing you may have to delete something you have kept is a deterrent to making hasty purchases.

Sarah loves wooden spoons because of their versatility. She kept three of her favorites to be sure one was always clean when she needed it. But she had a difficult time resisting a new one every time she passed the store displays with them. When she stopped to consider which one she would have to delete of her favorites, she decided against the new purchase every time.

The same principle applies to every new thing coming into you home and space. When you have taken the time and thought to keep something as you organize, would you want to let it go just to get a new one? Sorting that out in your mind can help you make good decisions and over time it becomes second nature.

• Rent or Borrow

Another question is to consider whether you could rent a new item or borrow it. Books can be checked out of libraries and movies can be rented. This habit is a great training tool for your children. They naturally love libraries and realizing borrowed items must be returned helps then learn time organizing skills.

Some purchases not only are expensive but consume too much space for their usefulness. If you only have a few carpets or rugs that seldom need deep cleaning, then renting a carpet shampooer would be a better choice than purchasing and storing one. The same would be true for the router tiller you need once a year for the vegetable garden or the 100 cup coffee maker for you daughter's graduation reception.

If per chance it really is less expensive to buy than rent but you need it only once or less than once a year, consider donating it after you have used it.

• Determine Its Home Beforehand

That ubiquitous question from my husband, "Where are you going to put it?" is really a good self check for determining if the item is worth destroying the attractive arrangement your organizing has created.

If you have to rearrange everything in the space to make room for the new item, just think about how much time and energy that will take. And you may be very disappointed in the results. How much is that new item really worth in the big picture?

• Just Say No—Yard Sales

In the attempt to get a great deal, we can be swept away by the pull of getting something for nearly nothing. Items scattered over a driveway and lawn beckon us to stop and just look.

If you have your list of things you really need in your possession, then you might be justified in stopping to check out what was there.

If not, then it is best to keep moving and realize that there but for the grace of God would be you trying to unload clutter on some unsuspecting soul.

As a side note, I must confess that my father, the yard sale junkie, outfitted my children with NFL jackets, Polly Flinders dresses and every riding toy imaginable. It was a retirement activity for him and a blessing to me, a stay at home mom at the time. So I am admitting the sales can be good if you stick to that needs list and resist what you really don't need and would clutter your homes.

• Just Say No—Thrift Stores

Thrift stores can trap us the same way. Thank God the stores that I use have their drop off baskets at the door so I can make my donation without having to peruse the isles of supposed bargains.

Unless you shop them everyday, the odds are you will not find the deal of the century there. It is the eBay and flea market sellers that are checking out the stores on a daily basis and making purchases to resell for a profit. I have seen them in action.

While standing in line to get my donation receipt one afternoon, I noticed a man in front of me making a purchase of some very nice but unrelated things. All of them were high end items I just happened to recognize. As I followed him out the door, I saw him get into his truck with a local flea market logo on it. He was making the purchases to resell.

Even with a needs list, it is hard to compete with that but if you have the time and are willing to stick with it, you may be able to find an item on your list. Otherwise, dismiss them as another trap to rob you of your freedom.

- ## Just Say No—Infomercials

   This topic has been discussed, but it needs to be stated again. Before you call and order anything you see advertised in long or short television commercials or on the shopping networks, do your homework. Check out the reviews from as many sources as possible.

   More than once I have been surprised at the negative reports from consumers who have used the products. Claims are exaggerated and even the demonstrations of the products are not accurate representations many times. Buyer beware is just as important here as anywhere.

- ## Just Say No—Sale of the Year

   One problem with all of those flyers than come into the house are the beckoning announcements of the greatest sales ever. Whether it is 30% off you entire purchases or half off the regular price, the enticement to save money on a purchase may be too much to ignore. Then there are the buy one get one free advertisements. Don't be persuaded to run out and stock up if you don't have the space.

   Once you enter the stores there are still more bargains too good to resist. My trap was always the clearance rack that contained the half off the lowest marked down price items. If a blouse was originally $80 and now it would be $6.50, how could I not buy it? The fabric to make it would cost more than that.

   The fact that it was orange with purple polka dots and would not coordinate with much less match anything in the closet was beside the point. It was just too good of deal to resist even if it would add more to my full closet. In his great words that I now know as wisdom, my father would also ask, "How could you be saving money when you just spent $6.50?" That is an excellent point and one I keep asking myself when tempted to make purchases that are not on my "need to buy" list.

• Walking the Malls

The genius that developed the first enclosed mall should have been given the Nobel Prize for Economics that year. With controlled climates, beautiful displays, bright lights, security guards and food courts, anyone can enjoy the shopping experience in complete comfort.

In fact, they are so nice that walking clubs have formed that use the local mall as a central place to register and keep track of their members' activity. I know because I was victim to it one year during my summer break from teaching.

Since it was my unpaid vacation, I did not want to get up at the crack of dawn. I would begin walking about 9:00 and finish about 10:00 each morning. Yes, that was just in time for the stores to open. The fact that my face was beet red and I was dripping sweat did not hinder my going into the stores. After all, I had looked at those store front displays with the bargain of the day 14 times doing my laps around and around the tile pathways.

The sales clerks did not seem to mind my exhausted appearance when I made my purchases and increased their commission for the day. It was a win-win situation for everything but my closet and budget. And they were not screaming freedom.

• Retail Therapy

Although shopping has become a social event for families and friends, it is in your best interest to find other ways to enjoy your time with them. Just like you know you should not go grocery shopping when you are hungry, you need to watch why you are shopping for other things.

Shopping when you are emotionally upset, frustrated, angry, bitter, resentful, sad or excited is not a good idea. You may buy items you do not need, may not be able to afford and will clutter you space.

Take a walk around the block rather than around the mall to release some of that tension. It will make you, your pocketbook and your space feel free.

• Cold Turkey Shopping

After all of your hard work, you should not allow yourself to be lured into the trap of finding great deals you just can't resist just because they are a great deal. As good as they may be, they can unravel you organizing hard work very quickly.

This does not mean that you can never enjoy shopping again, but using the cold turkey approach for several months can help break any old bad habits you may have had.

Learn to keep a list of items you really need and stick to it when shopping for food, clothes, toiletries, etc. Eventually the thought of buying items just because they are a great deal will be repulsive to you. As hard as that is to believe right now, trust me it can happen. The longer you are persistent in saying no to non essential items, the greater your freedom will be.

The Gift Dilemma

Americans are a generous people. We love expressing our appreciation and celebrating with gifts. The commercial market has maximized that spirit by making the most of every holiday including Grandparents Day (It is in September.) with appropriate cards, etc. We love to give and we love to receive.

I think it is very important to teach children to be generous in giving but also gracious in receiving. Every gift should be acknowledged with a thank you note. The sooner you write the note the better, but no matter how long after receiving it, it must be acknowledged.

Once you have thanked the giver, the dilemma of what to do with a gift can become a space problem if it is not consumable. Unless it is from your children or parents, especially in-law children or parents, you are free to do with it as you please. (For good advice on relationships with in-laws, I recommend *Just Call Me Mom* by Mary Tatem.)

Gifts that you do not use and want or do not have the space to display can be returned for credit or donated to a good cause. Missy, the young military wife, donated gift baskets of cosmetic items to a young girl down the street who wanted to be a cosmetician. She was thrilled to get them and Missy was delighted to pass them on to someone who wanted them.

Letting those close to you know you would like gifts that do not clutter in the future is a good idea. If they are aware of your organizing journey, they will be respectful of you wishes and not offended. In fact, you can set that example yourself and give others clutter free gifts. Some examples are listed here.

CLUTTER FREE GIFTS

Women

Outdoor plants
Fresh flowers
Day Spa coupons
Lotions, soaps

Cleaning, chore coupons

Car wash coupons

Help with decluttering

Printed paper napkins

Label Maker

Wooden hangers

Drawer organizers

Babysitting coupon

Basket of teas, coffees

Men

Fishing, hunting license

Round of golf

Tickets to games

Oil changes

Yard work coupons

Car wash, detailing service/coupons

Garage cleaning coupon

Computer software

Blockbuster certificates

Children

Memberships to zoo, park, museum

Cookie decorating day

Puppet washcloths

Pool passes

Theme park passes or tickets

Coupons for bowling

Anyone

Favorite store gift certificates

Tickets to movies, opera, theater

Registration for a class

Paper shredder

Memberships

Season passes

Landscaping, garden certificates

Restaurant certificates

Bread, jams and jellies

Cookies, cakes

Lessons for exercise, sports

Donations to charity in their name

Weekend getaway

Overnight at a Bed and Breakfast

Professional Organizer Coupons

Is Cleanliness Next to Orderliness?

Being organized and being clean are not synonymous but they are obviously related. It is difficult to clean a space when it is disorganized but one can be organized without having the space sanitized.

It is interesting that uncluttered spaces appear to be cleaner than cluttered spaces. It is a good idea to keep visible surfaces as uncluttered as possible to make them more visually pleasing. Think about it as you look around a room. Is it dust or grime that you see first or cluttered floors or furnishings?

There is a family I know whose husband is the whole house organizer and his wife is the whole house sanitizer. Nick folds the laundry because his clothes must fit in their spaces efficiently, but a little dust is no problem for him. Sarah on the other hand would allow items to accumulate around the sink, but the counter would be continually wiped down with disinfectant.

Together they have learned to adapt to each other and you never need to worry about their home being ready for visitors at a moment's notice. There is no doubt the onset of children will change things with them (and all the mothers said AMEN), but I digress and will continue that topic later on.

But Cleanliness is Good

I don't want you to think cleanliness is not important. Keeping surfaces clean can help deter the spread of disease and allergies can be helped by eliminating as much of the dust particles as possible. And things just look better when they are clean as well as organized.

If you have children attending a day care or school, you are aware of the plethora of viruses and bacteria that can invade your house. From experience I can tell you teaching 150 germ carrying students a day will build up your immunity like no flu vaccine ever will. (If you don't teach, volunteer. It may work the same way.)

It is important to understand that stacking and piling up items or having bags and boxes of things sitting for extended periods of time can lead to mold and mildew on wall and floors. They also invite insects and varmints which can invade the spaces without realizing what has happened. Eventually these can damage property and cause illness.

Eliminating clutter and organizing spaces as well as keeping spaces clean are important to your health. It is good to have both.

Hoarding

Unfortunately when spaces become extremely disorganized, it is difficult to keep a cleaning and maintenance routine. Then the environment can spiral downhill into unsanitary conditions. We have seen television programs and read articles featuring the deplorable conditions in the homes of hoarders and wonder how a living space could get that way.

To begin understanding hoarding, you need to realize such situations did not happen overnight. Little by little and over time items accumulated until cleaning was impossible and attempts at improvement became overwhelming.

Hoarders never planned for the situation to get that way and the conditions are devastating to all involved. The scriptural admonition to "judge not lest you be judged" is certainly applicable here. Most hoarders are kind, loving and sensitive people. They often want to change so the appropriate action for us to take is to point them to those resources that can help them. Those are listed in the resource section.

Help with Maintenance

Maintaining your spaces is much easier when they are organized. Cleaning floors is faster when nothing is piled on them, furniture can be clean when you don't have to shuffle excess items around and spaces just look cleaner.

Keeping spaces organized is not a one person affair unless you live alone. It means everyone in the family will have to be on board in order for changes to be permanent. It is not a simple thing to do, but the results are so worth it. Often family members are so pleased with the newly organized spaces that they are motivated to keep it that way.

Sometimes life events can alter our maintenance schedules. Some of those were mentioned earlier. When that happens, additional help may be needed to keep things running. Do not be hesitant to rally the troops and let others pitch in as needed.

Hire help if necessary, but delegate tasks to children and spouses also. You may barter services with a friend or develop new routines. Whatever works best for you is what you need to put in place. Just don't wait so long that frustration sets in and you lose hope.

Managing What You Have

Some of our things need continual maintenance. As we go through the chapters relating to specific spaces, we will offer strategies that will help you keep your organized spaces attractive and functional. This is a commitment you will have to make as you break old habits and learn new ones.

Getting a place organized is not enough to maintain an orderly environment. It is an ongoing process that we all must engage on a daily basis. We will backslide from time to time as our situation changes, but a desire to keep our systems in place is the best motivator to compel us to get back on track.

None of us are perfect and we do not have perfect homes if we live in them. But we want them to be functional and attractive. It is easier to do that when they and we are organized.

Maintenance and Cleaning Tips

- Keep a needs list of items you must have.
- Keep as much off the floor as possible. It makes cleaning much easier.
- Keep a donate bag for items to be passed on and carry them away every week.
- Keep a wastebasket in every room and empty it often.

- Vacuum rather than dust if time is limited. It makes the area look better.
- Use attractive but washable fabrics to cover wood furniture so they do not have to be dusted. (tablecloths, dresser scarves, table toppers, small quilts, even wall hangings)
- Have a daily pick up routine that everyone knows.
- Clean the most obvious messes first.
- Make your bed as soon as you get out of it. The last one out makes it.
- As you leave a room, turn around and look to see if it is clutter free.
- Learn to love clutter free counters and table tops.
- Plan long range maintenance tasks so they are not forgotten.
- Use positive self talk when doing mundane tasks.
- Get help by being specific. Say "pick up your Lego's" rather than "clean your room."
- Get and maintain the proper tools for cleaning.
- Invest in basic supplies: glass cleaner, degreaser, soft cloths and abrasive pads.
- Clean the bathroom from the cleanest area to the dirtiest, usually top to floor.
- If space allows, keep basic cleaning supplies at each sink. If not, carry a tote.
- Beautify what you clean with flowers and polish.

THE EMERGENCY CLEAN UP/ORGANIZING SCHEDULE

We all get caught off guard from time to time and find ourselves facing unexpected visitors or guests in a short amount of time. This schedule will help you prepare for that as much as possible in about an hour.

- **Think and Plan—5 minutes.** Think about which rooms will be used and what items you will need. Usually not all rooms will be needed. If it is a teenage sleepover, plans are different than your husband's boss. Make a list of where you need to work and what you will need to get.

- **Clear the Entrances—5 minutes.** Make the outside and inside of the house entrance look as neat and clean as possible. This is the first impression your guests will have. Pick up any toys, papers, etc. that may be on the sidewalk or porch. Quickly clean the glass window if you have one. Light a scented candle in the foyer.

- **Clean the Bathroom—10 minutes.** No matter who comes in, they will eventually go to the bathroom to freshen up. Wipe down all the visible surfaces, polish the mirror and fixtures and put out fresh towels and soap. Don't forget to flush the toilet, especially if you have little children.

- **Pick up Trash—5 minutes.** Use a trash bag and go to each of the rooms you identified in step 1. Empty the trash cans into the bag while you are there.

- **Collect the Clutter—15 minutes.** Use a laundry basket to pick up large items that are out of place. Return them to their homes if you have remaining time. Otherwise, set it in an out of the way place. It is an open container so you will not forget about it later on. Use an open container such as a dishpan, basket or box to pick up smaller items. If papers are outdated, recycle them. Return the items to their homes.

- **Make a Quick Clean Sweep—10 minutes.** Clean the floors first. Use a floor sweeper if you have one as it will go from carpet to other floors effectively. Dust mop or sweep if that is more efficient. Dust the furniture with a micro fiber, treated or damp cloth.

- **Freshen the Room and Yourself—10 minutes**. Use lighting and music to set whatever mood you need. Add plants or flowers if you have them available. Make nice table arrangements with vases, candles, trays, folded napkins, etc. Put on a clean top and brush your hair. Touch up your make up and spray cologne if you like it. Take a deep breath and roll you head from side to side. Roll your shoulders from front to back. Relax and promise yourself you will make a plan to keep yourself better prepared for the next time. Smile as you go to the door.

PART THREE
Solutions for Organizing Specific Spaces

Chapter 11

PAPERWORK AND MAIL

aper in the form of mail, schedules, bulletins, flyers, lists, magazines, newspapers and catalogues to mention a few creates one of the most significant sources of disorganization in the home or office. Stacks of it can form so quickly that a problem can develop as to what to do with it. About half of my organizing business deals with creating systems to control and manage it.

TOO MUCH OF IT

We were lured into the world of computers thinking it would save us from so much paper but we soon came to realize it did not. Before we became so addicted to e-mail messages (that we now print), we had telephone calls that required no paper. We might have taken notes on a memo pad or the back of an envelope if we were desperate, but we would not have used an entire sheet of copy paper for it.

In addition we print documents off the Internet that we think are important and will go away if we turn off our computer. And we also print our own files, calendars, etc. So the computer age did not help us, and we still have a paper problem.

Think about this. If just 5 pieces of paper come into your life everyday and you only dispose of 1, at the end of a year you would have almost 1500 sheets of paper to sort or organize. Do that for 2 or more years and you have quite a stash to handle.

It Requires Too Much

Like the unwanted relative or neighbor's kid, papers just keep coming and coming and coming to us and we have to do something with them. They require time to sort and decisions must be made about each piece.

Do we keep it or let it go? Do we read it before we let it go? If we choose to let it go, how do we get rid of it? If we keep it, where do we put it, when will we put it there and will we be able to find it again? And this process happens day after day. There is just too much paper in our lives.

Paper Procrastination

Yes, we can procrastinate with just about anything including paper. If we don't take the time and energy to make decisions about the papers and indiscriminately set them down, piles of it will accumulate. This makes it almost impossible to find the one piece you may need in the future.

Delores was a busy mom of five children ages 5 to 19. Lots of mail came into her house but she had no system for handling it. As a result she would allow it to stack on the kitchen counter until she needed the space or visitors were coming. Her method of dealing with them at that point was to scoop them up into a plastic grocery store bag. Then she would drop them in an upstairs closet or another out of the way place.

Months and even a couple of years had passed before she pulled all of the bags into an empty room for us to sort. Sadly we were unable to find a missing tuition check that had been sent to her oldest child.

It Becomes Clutter and Mutates

Mail and other papers have the unique attribute of not only stacking up and becoming clutter but mutating into other types of clutter. Let's go back to the earlier comments about the dining room table.

In many households the family has an eat in kitchen and then a formal or separate dining room with a wonderful, flat, large horizontal space called the dining room table. In other homes it may be the kitchen counter that catches items. It is just asking for something to be put on it. And most often the answer is paper.

It usually starts as a stack of mail dropped as one enters the house. After removing a coat, letting the dog out for a break and checking the answering machine, you might get around to looking through the pile. If nothing requires your immediate attention, you leave the stack there and move on.

This could happen for a couple of days and then you come home from a shopping spree and the phone rings as you enter the door. The bags go down with the papers since it already has stacked items and a little more won't hurt. Then little Johnny comes home with his graded science project and sets it with the stacks.

The mutating has begun and will continue until the next special event requiring a neat, clean house and an empty table or counter appears on the schedule. Panic hits and the papers and all of its breeding are bagged, boxed or removed in some manner. I cannot count on my fingers, toes and freckles how many times I have been called in to help with the dining room table or counter dilemma. And it all started with papers.

A PAPER SYSTEM

All papers need a system for handling and storage. No matter how simple or complex, a system should work for you so that there are no loose papers floating around. And you should be able to find the one you need in less than a minute. Yes, that is possible.

Most clients with a paper management dilemma already have their own system that isn't working. It would be nice if we could start with a new system and begin the management with all the new papers. Unfortunately that would not take care of the papers already there. In those cases we can set up a system but the old and incoming papers must be incorporated into it. This can appear to create more disorganization at the beginning. But you must start somewhere. My approach is to keep it as simple as possible so it is easy to set up, use and maintain for the rest of your life.

Reduce the Amount of Incoming Papers

There are as many kinds of systems for paper organization as there are people that need them, but they all have common principles and similar tools or supplies. These include limiting the number of papers coming into your mailbox and house. When there is less coming in there is obviously less to manage.

• Unsolicited Mail

Our wonderful world of bulk mail has made it possible for you to see many of the great opportunities for spending your money. Advertisers have found there are victims out there or they would not keep using it.

If you are annoyed by commercials that interrupt you favorite television programs, you should be just as annoyed at bulk mail that enters your house and interrupts your time to read it and space to keep it. It is another thief entering your house to steal your time, money and space.

An important strategy in reducing the paper dilemma is to throw out any mail that does not have your name on it. You can reduce the amount of advertisements you receive with your name on it by contacting agencies that will take you name off the direct mail distribution lists. That information is located in the resource section. Be sure to list every possible way your name could be printed on an address label.

A flyer may have the greatest bargain of the century in it, but if it does, you will find out about it another way. And sorting through all of it to find that one coupon that will likely expire before you use it is just not a good investment of your time, energy and space. Get over it and put them and anything else with the word occupant, neighbor, family or resident on the label in the recycle bin.

• Coupons

I must digress here on the topic of coupons. If you are one of those efficient coupon organizers, and I know some personally so I know you are out there, then by all means find and keep the coupons, but if you are not good at already managing those money saving papers, then wait until you have a good paper handling system before you add that to your organizing. There is no condemnation to those who do or do not use coupons.

Personally, I have not joined that group because I always had a job or two going on that took up the time coupons demanded. I could teach or sort coupons, professionally organize or sort coupons, be a room mother or sort coupons, but I could not do all of those things. Coupons lost out when ever there was a choice of activities. If you can manage coupons effectively, then God bless you and go for it. It can be a great money saving strategy. But if you do not, go in peace and with less paper.

• Magazines

Some of the abundance of mail we get is what we asked for. Magazines we don't get around to reading are one of them. I became the victim of quilting magazines. I loved getting them because they had beautiful pictures of quilts with the patterns to do them. After they stacked up for a few months without being read much less used for making quilts, I realized I was wasting my money and space on them.

You may have cooking magazines that you ordered because you thought you would try out some new recipes. If you haven't done it in a month or two, you probably never will. The same goes for golfing or fishing techniques in magazines. Anything you really need to know about any topic is on the Internet and if you don't have a computer, your library does. It also has magazines you can read while you are there.

If you do actually read the magazines, save only the current issue and pass on the older ones. If you find you are getting behind, scan the table of contents and tear out the articles you want to read. Put them in a folder in the car and pull them out when you are waiting in a doctor's office, in the car for the train to pass or stalled traffic to begin moving again.

If your child is selling magazines for the school, scouts, etc. feel free to purchase them if you have the available funds. Then have them sent to someone in a nursing home, to a medical office or other suitable address. When I took Linda to the urgent care center there was not a magazine in the entire facility. I understand patients walk out with them so you might consider donating all of you back issues to facilities like that.

Cutting down on the number of subscriptions you receive or better yet eliminating them all together will save money and make more space in your home. It is an easy way to create freedom.

• Catalogues

Catalogues fall into a similar category. I love going online to do my shopping. It saves me time and money in many ways, but it does create the inevitable influx of catalogues in my outdoor mailbox. Once the retailer has your address to deliver the items, it has it to deliver the catalogues, sale brochures, flyers and more. And by now you realize catalogues are one very long commercial whose aim is to get you to spend money.

You can spend hours flipping through the pages to get to the one item you might be interested in buying. This does not include the money you might spend on items you really don't need or had not even considered purchasing before it arrived.

If you are in the market for a product, go to that page and tear it out to order later. If you have a specific need for an item you can also cut out any online code or the in store discount coupon and save it for when you are shopping. Toss the rest of the catalogue, etc. in the recycle bin.

Keep Your Information Private

Be very selective in giving out your phone number or address. Many retailers now ask for you phone number at the register where you make your purchase. That gives them enough information to find you address and begin sending you advertisements. A simple reply of, "No, please, that number is private," is all you need to say.

Warranty cards for purchases are not required to be completed and mailed for your guarantee to be valid. And have you ever noticed all of the unrelated questions they ask on the attached survey? That is strictly to enable them to sell your information. Keeping your receipt and any warranty information in your files is all that you need to be covered by it.

You may even request that only your name be listed in the local phone book. This has a trickle down effect of reducing the amount of bulk mail you receive. I have even seen a reduction in my bulk mail since my phone numbers were added to the national Do Not Call listing. The information for that service is also in the resource section.

Consolidate Accounts

The more financial and credit accounts you have, the more mail you will get. Consolidating as many of those as you can eliminates a considerable amount of incoming papers. Many of those institutions also sell your address to others who will add more mail to your box.

Consider making all of your credit purchases on one or two cards that give you reward points. Several of my clients have earned free gifts, travel and nights in hotels with their points. One couple had enough hotel points for their children and grandchildren to attend a family reunion in another state.

Pay Bills Online

Paying bills online has become one of the most effective ways to manage accounts. It also eliminates the need to save all of the extra papers and envelopes that come with the statement. You have more control than you think with online banking including verification that your bills were paid on time. The bank will go to bat for you if your payment is challenged.

With each payment you set the amount you want paid to each account and the date you want it sent. Every person I know who uses online banking is glad they did because of the time, money and space it saves them.

Control Children's Papers

Some of the incoming papers are not mail. This includes Johnny's artwork and graded papers that he is anxious for you to see. (We will discuss children's things more in Chapter 13.) It is important that you let him describe each one to you and then have him pick out the one thing he would like for you to display. Allowing him to choose will keep him happy as you discard the remaining papers he brought home.

You will want to replace the older paper displayed with the new one. Displaying only one paper at a time is a good organizing strategy and teaches the child how to make choices.

If there are some special papers that he wants to keep forever, create a box for them. Flat scrapbook paper containers or large pizza boxes are good for this. When it is full, allow him to purge what he is willing to let go. A lifetime of memories can be held in that box. It should be stored in his room.

Another choice is to take a picture of the child with his paper and keep the photo but not the paper. The photo can be stored digitally thus eliminating the paper problem.

Of course you should save the paper he wrote on why you are his favorite person or the Valentine he made just for you, but pages of practicing the letter "p" in cursive should not be one of the saved items that can mutate into clutter.

There are other important papers that might come in the backpack. Notices of upcoming events, lunch menus for the week and homework assignments may be included in those papers. Many of those items can be found on the school and teacher's websites for future reference or the information can be transferred to a message center or incoming paper box that is discussed later on.

WATCH MISCELLANEOUS PAPERS

It is obvious children have their share of papers, but we bring in lots of them too. Church bulletins, garden club schedules, office work, course notes, conference handouts, etc. all make their way into the house with our own bodies. It is a good strategy to take a moment or two before we collect or pack up those papers to think about what we will do with them once we are inside our homes.

Some papers will be essential and they should have their own designated space when they arrive in the house. Everything in your house needs a specific home, even papers. If you cannot think of a place they will go before you arrive, then reconsider if you really need them.

Managing the Incoming Papers

As papers enter the house they need a place to go. This may be a trial and error process as you find a system that works for you. You need to get any members of the family that handle papers on board with this process.

Places and Supplies for Papers

Papers need a specific place in the house to be sorted and kept when they come in. One suggestion I give clients is to try to find a place near to where you would normally drop it after you enter the house. It may be a kitchen counter, a foyer table, the infamous dining room table or by the phone.

While you want it to be convenient, you don't want it to be in the way of how you normally use that space. If you have extensive kitchen counters, then it would be okay to continue to put papers there. If you have limited counter space then it might be better to find a space close by but not on the counters.

Supplies you may need include:

- Incoming Paper Container/File—a vertical file box, the size depends on the activities of the family
- Hanging folders
- Waste basket
- Recycling bin
- Paper shredder

An Incoming Paper Container/File

The most positive feedback I get in helping clients organize their papers is my recommendation to install a vertical file for incoming papers. It is a very good organizing tool and I will elaborate on it because of its effectiveness.

- To be the most successful, it should contain vertical hanging folders labeled with the categories pertaining to the papers most often needing sorting. For those who like to stack their papers horizontally so they can see them, I will reassure you that you will be able to see these papers, too.
- The tabs of the hanging folders should be labeled with the categories most needed in sorting the incoming papers. For my clients I start with several basic labels:

  Bills To Pay

  Respond/Do

  To File

Read

Receipts

Coupons

Names of persons in the family that might receive mail

Names of specific activities that generate papers such as scouts, church, school, work, etc. Each family will have its own special categories.

- The size and style of the container would depend on the amount of papers and the location for it. If it will be out in the open for the whole world to see, I recommend an attractive office style box or one covered in pretty paper or fabric.

  Missy found a paper covered hanging file that had a lid. She sorted mail on her kitchen counter that was opened to the large family room where she entertained guest. When she knew visitors would be arriving, she put the lid on the box to keep her papers private and to make it more attractive.

  Others keep the container at their message centers so that all of the communication tools are in one place.

- There are many styles of hanging folders that can be used. I prefer those that have more permanent style tabs such as Ready Tab by Pendaflex and Fast Tab by Smead. These folders also come in a variety of colors to make sorting faster for those who prefer color coding.

- If you choose not to use hanging folders, other folders can be used in containers that would be more acceptable to you. I would recommend using pocket folders with a box bottom placed in containers with no dividers. Examples of those containers would be dishpans or similarly shaped baskets or boxes.

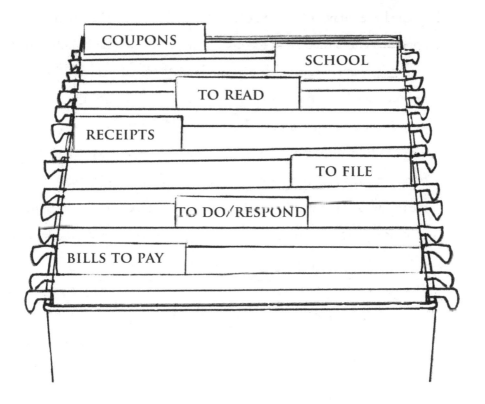

Sample Incoming Paper File Box

Sorting the Saved Incoming Papers

With your sorting box located conveniently, make a decision about each piece of paper that comes into the house.

- **The Bills to Pay folder** is self explanatory. Any statements coming in are left there until it is time to make the payments. Then the folder can be emptied and the bills paid. You never have to worry about lost bills again.

- **The Respond/Do folder** is used for notices of upcoming events, invitations to weddings or parties, reminders to schedule appointments or notes for tasks you need to do. This file should be opened everyday. Once the event has been put on the calendar, the appointment is made and recorded, the party attendance confirmed, etc. those papers can be disposed. If they contain travel directions or other pertinent information, they can be saved until the event has passed or the activity accomplished.

- **The "To File" folder** should be very temporary. It holds items that need to be filed in a reference or permanent file cabinet. This might include the renewed auto insurance policy, correspondence from an accountant or attorney, etc. To prevent them from getting lost in a stack, file them with the incoming papers and purge that file on schedule.

- **The Read folder** can contain articles, newsletters or correspondence you will want to read later on. Do not take the time to do this while you are sorting. After reading the material, make a decision as to whether you want to file it more permanently or dispose of it. Most information based articles can be found online.

- **The Receipts folder** can hold any receipts you bring in the house from purchases. They are in a safe place with easy access if you need to verify a credit card statement or return an item for refund or exchange. Once its usefulness is no longer valid, destroy it. If you have eaten the food and did not get sick or have worn the dress 10 times, you no longer have a reason to save those receipts.

I understand that some states require receipts for validation of sales tax deductions on income taxes. For those clients I recommend scanning the receipts with any computer software. Neat Receipts is a software application designed specifically for this. It is also useful when receipts are needed for other accounting applications.

Many receipts are now printed on thermal paper and the information fades over time. This makes it even more important to have a place to put them until they can be processed for permanent storage.

- **The Coupons folder** would contain any coupons arriving at the house. We have already discussed the coupon issue and having a temporary file for those can make the sorting and saving process easier. They will not be mixed in with other papers and can be retrieved when needed. .

- **Folders for specific activities and persons** in the family are self explanatory, too. You will know when to add more categories and what to put in them as the need arises. Resist the urge to make a miscellaneous category as a catch all. It can become filled with items that should be disposed.

Processing the Incoming Papers

As papers come into the house, they should be immediately sorted. Having a shredder, trash can and recycle bin nearby makes the process easier. As you sort you must decide if you want to keep, shred, recycle or trash them. Follow local guidelines for proper removal of all types of papers.

- Shred any papers with personal information that needs to be removed.

- Do not keep papers if you can find the information on them elsewhere.

- Do not take the time to read through each paper. Sort all of them first and then go back to those you wish to read thoroughly.

- Do not over think your decisions. The more you practice using the purging options, the easier it gets. Clients tell me all the time that they can toss catalogues and flyers now without even opening them. I call that a real time and space saver. I call it freedom.

- For the remaining papers, file them in the appropriate category and set a schedule for purging them. The time you pay bills, the first of the month or a specific date each month should be decided and then stick to it.

Message Centers

A central place for family communication is called a message center. It is the perfect place to locate incoming papers since it is convenient and available to everyone. The types of containers or files for those papers are described in the next section.

Just about any space can be configured into a message center. The end of the kitchen counter, a desk in the family room or an empty wall where you could install a shelf or two might work for your family. Some are located in cabinets where the shelves and inside of the door are used to consolidate the items.

A large family calendar that is easily visible is almost a necessity for all families. It can be used to record dates of meetings, events and appointments so the paper notices can be recycled.

A message board for attaching notes or a dry erase board for writing notes can be added to contain details of events or personal notes to family members. These should be religiously updated so that they remain attractive and the information on them does not become background wallpaper in the space.

If a Household Notebook described below is used, then it could be placed in the message center, too.

The location of a phone and/or computer in the message center adds to the convenience of maintaining communication. It is not necessary if space is limited but can be considered if you are planning a new message center.

The message center may also be the place for the family business/management office. A home business office might be located there, too. Depending on the size of the house, the amount of space and the family needs, this area may have many or just a few uses.

The Household Notebook

If the incoming paper container becomes filled with items that cannot be purged often, you may want to consider a household notebook.

This is a three ring binder that contains categories of papers that are needed on a more permanent basis. Some examples are school menus, sports schedules, frequently used contact information, rosters, children's chore charts, family menu schedules, reminders for household maintenance and repeating events such as holidays, birthdays and other special occasions, etc. If plastic page protectors are used, loose recipes or articles can be stored in them.

Johnny may have a soccer game on March 10th and you have put it on the family calendar but there is not room there to write the name of the field for the game, or if he wears a home or visitor jersey. The schedule with all of those details can be put in the household notebook.

When it is placed in a family message center, the notebook becomes a very important communication tool and a convenient way to keep those more permanent papers.

If no center exists, the notebook can be placed in the incoming paper file box since most are about the size of a hanging folder. This option may require a deeper container for the folders and notebook to be located together.

Suggestions for using the notebook, printable calendars and forms as well as possible categories to be included can be found online. That information is given in the resource section.

Managing Reference or Permanent Papers

Some papers need to be kept for future reference or documentation. I call these reference files. Those documents that are of a legal nature or should be kept indefinitely I call permanent files. These are normally the papers we file in folders in a file cabinet, file box, desk file drawer or rolling cart with a filing bin. It seems that the longer you live, the more papers and files you accumulate and keep. At some point most of us come to the realization that you cannot keep all of them forever.

• Reference Files

Most papers that are stored as reference files are those that may be useful to you in the future. We are listing some of the categories we often use in filing those papers. It should be noted now that some of these categories would contain original documents or papers that may be kept indefinitely in more secure locations and some in emergency boxes. We will discuss those later. Depending on your situation, copies of these documents can also be kept in the reference files as listed here.

Appliances and Equipment	Household Furnishings
Auto and Vehicles	Insurance
Banking and Credit	Investments and Saving
Bills, Paid	Legal Records
Correspondence	Miscellaneous
Contacts	Medical Information
Employment Records	Organizations
Financial Information	Pets
Housing	Tax Returns/Documents

Within these categories you would include file folders that contain the specific papers you are keeping. You may find you could delete some of these but need other categories. These should be personalized to your situation but need to be broad so they can be easily located For example some of my clients have a category for pets where they keep veterinary records, city license information, pet insurance policies, breeding records, etc. Others could eliminate that category from their files.

- ## Reference Files Supplies

Reference papers should be kept in a file cabinet, drawer or box designed for them. Whatever the style, it should provide rails for using hanging folders. These hanging folders keep papers from sliding into a pile or crammed in so tightly that accessing them is difficult. As discussed earlier, those with permanent tabs are the most desirable.

Reference papers are placed in manila folders that are designed to fit in the hanging folder. It is important that these manila folders should have labels that briefly but adequately describe its contents.

Using nouns first with an adjective following is the most effective way to do this. For example the repair records for a Ford truck would be placed in the Auto/Vehicle category in a folder labeled Repairs-Ford. If there were more than one Ford in the household, it could be Repairs-Ford Truck. Another option would be to list the Ford first then Repairs. Either way, it would be easy to determine what is in that folder.

THE FILING PROCESS

There is a very effective way to go quickly to these categories and find the files in them. This is not original with me but I began using it years ago and think it is an excellent strategy that you can use. There are no added expenses of purchasing special supplies or the more complicated systems available on the market today.

- All category tabs are labeled on a hanging folder on the same side of the folder. So either all label tabs for the categories are on the left side of the hanging folders or all tabs for the categories are on the right side of the hanging folders. The categories cannot be labeled on both sides in the same cabinet, box or drawer.

- The specific manila folders containing the papers will only be labeled on the center tab of a folder or a tab on the opposite side from the category tab.

- All of the manila folders in one category are placed in alphabetical order behind their category tab on the hanging folder. Since this is a dynamic system and papers can change, it is impossible to exactly rotate the manila folders from center to side evenly. As long as they are in alphabetical order it really doesn't matter.

What is so effective about this system is how quickly you can find the category since they are the only tabs on that side and you don't have to flip through a bunch of manila folders to find them. Once in the correct category, these folders can be quickly located as they are kept alphabetically.

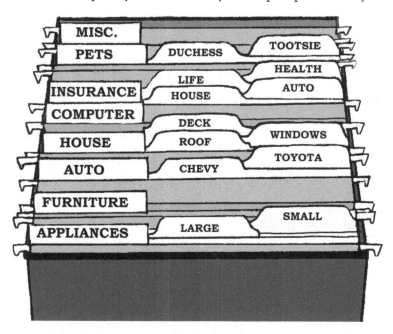

Sample Reference Files

Helpful Hints for Filing

- Use staples rather than paper clips for papers. Paper clips tend to catch on other papers.

- Label folders with a fine tip permanent marker or label maker for easy reading.

- Creating a separate index of your files may help in keeping up with what you have.

- Maintain and evaluate the papers in your manila folders at least once a year.

- Try not to overfill one folder. Divide the contents when it starts to bulge.

- Color code tabs, labels or folders if that is something that would help you.

- You may need several hanging folders behind the category folder to manage your manila folders. Do not label these additional hanging folders but only the manila folders inserted in them.

- Reference papers may contain recent statements, receipts, instruction booklets, copies of legal documents, warranties, policies, etc.

- Leave empty spaces in file drawers, boxes or cabinets for ease of use and placement of any additional folders in the future.

RETENTION GUIDELINES FOR PERSONAL RECORDS

The following are some guidelines to keep in mind when deciding whether to keep or toss papers. These are only suggestions. Remember that rules for retaining papers vary by state, industry, and individual practice. Talk to your attorney, accountant, or other knowledgeable source for guidance. You may also refer to the IRS retention guidelines at www.irs.gov

For Short Term Storage

Do keep some documents on a short-term basis unless they have been contested or could be needed for documentation later on. Those items should be saved until the need is gone.

- Monthly statements or bills such as from credit bureaus, utility companies, automobile installment payments or other financial records are needed for verification only.

- These can be destroyed after verification since most records are kept on file with the institution.

- If you insist on keeping them, at the end of the year, staple together by type and store elsewhere until they are no longer needed—not more than one year.

- Important correspondence can be saved until no longer necessary, usually less than a year.

For Long-Term Storage

Keep these records 3 to 7 years. Review periodically according to professional advice:

- End of the year bank and other financial statements or payments
- Uncomplicated and unchallenged tax returns with documentation
- Large purchase records including cancelled checks and/or receipts
- Expired contracts, insurance policies
- Repair and maintenance records for buildings, property

Permanent, Legal and Vital Records

Keep the following records forever or at least indefinitely in a safe place. Consider making copies for storage elsewhere or in a fireproof/waterproof box or both.

Included are personal records of legal value:

- Birth certificates
- Death certificates

- Marriage license or certificates
- Divorce decree
- Adoption papers
- Custody agreements
- Citizenship/naturalization
- Military records
- Social Security cards
- Property titles or deeds
- Settlements,
- Last will and testaments,
- Powers of attorney, etc.
- Tax returns and supporting documents that were filed late, challenged, unpaid or part of other transactions.
- Property records
- Contracts
- Deeds
- Mortgages
- Appraisals
- Improvement records
- After selling, keep records at least seven years, closing statements indefinitely

Other permanent records include:
- Insurance policies (if it is no longer in force, keep records for at least five years)
- Investment records (if the asset is sold, keep summary records to support tax records)
- Pension plans
- Profit-sharing plans

- Benefit plans
- End of the year payroll statements (for verifying Social Security payments)
- Health and medical history and current insurance information
- Legal claims and litigation
- Patents, trademarks, and copyrights

NOTE: Household item manuals and receipts until equipment is no longer in use

Emergency Files

It is important to have legal documents stored in a safety deposit box, an attorney's office or with relatives in case of property destruction at your home. Copies of those may be kept in your reference files for information purposes.

The fireproof/waterproof boxes are effective but very heavy and in emergencies may be difficult to carry. I recommend having copies of important documents in a more portable container that can be picked up quickly if an emergency occurs. This includes copies of credit cards and the information for them.

Computer Files

Most of the important documents can also be scanned and stored into computer files and on portable disks. In addition, the files can be stored in online sites that are accessed with passwords for privacy.

These options provide additional levels of security and safety for documents and files. Check out and compare the fees for the online services if you think they may be a good choice for you.

Managing Computer Files

While it is not necessarily paper management, computer files do represent some of the paper files we have or take the place of those paper files. Managing those is important since locating a file you need in a timely manner is an organizational process. More information on storing and managing them can be found with your computer and software booklets.

Word Processing Documents and Files

Work you have stored in the form of files from word processing software should be stored in folders containing similar topics. If you have only one or two such files, they can remain in a general folder. If that folder gets large, you should consider creating another folder to contain additional files.

I do not recommend storing folders within folders within folders. This can become very confusing when trying to locate a file. Most operating systems have a general My Documents folder. Within that you can place other folders, but I would not go any further than that. If necessary create another general folder for your desktop.

Purging files you no longer need is another important process in keeping those you need easier to find.

Name your documents with words that easily identify your content. Adding the date in some form may help separate and identify similar documents.

Data and Accounting Files

These files should be categorized in the same manner as word processing files.

They usually have special identifying icons, extensions or labels so they are easily recognized. They take up much more storage space than word processing files so they should be reviewed for purging more often.

E-mail Accounts and Messages

We are addicted to e-mail and read messages as if they were letters from loved ones far away. To manage the accounts and messages, you must have some guidelines and stick with them. I recommend the following for maximizing your time and message folders.

- Create more than one e-mail account for your messages. You should have as many accounts as you need to help make accessing your messages less time consuming. I have a business blog with Google, a personal account with my domain name, a Juno account for my purchases, and a Yahoo account for my Faithful Organizers group.

  There are many free accounts available for you so I recommend you use only one account for those messages from people you want to send you messages.

  Create another account to use for online shopping and messages from commercial companies. You can check the status of your orders, print receipts and send comments from that account.

- Delete any forwarded messages unless you are sure they are worth reading.
- Check out any forwarded messages before you send it to anyone. This is especially true of warnings and alerts. Snopes and Urban Legends are two Internet sources you can use to do this. Their addresses are in the resource section at the end of this book. Even if they say it has been verified, check it out for yourself anyway.
- If you do read the forwarded notice and you have verified that it is a rumor or false, you should notify those who were sent the message with a "reply to all". Send them a message of your findings including the Internet source and paste the URL where you got your information. They can verify it on their own.

Include an exhortation to all that they should check things out before they send them. This will usually stop the person who sent you the message from doing it again. Dozens of people have thanked me for correcting false information they have received this way. If we were all diligent in taking these steps, it may reduce the amount of false messages out there.

- Use folders to store messages that you want to keep. This is better than printing them but you should not save everything. You can create and name as many folders as you need to identify the messages but try to keep the categories broad as you would with paper files.

- Copy and paste important messages into word processing files rather than printing them if you need permanent storage for them.

- Check your messages only two or three times a day and keep your reply as brief as possible. It will save you and the reader time. This is not the place for long letters unless it is you only form of communication. Use the phone for those who enjoy chatty conversations but set a timer so you will know when to stop.

Chapter 12

BEDROOMS
AND CLOTHING

While disorganized papers can be a visual problem for many areas in the home, bedrooms and clothing are usually kept out of sight. Since out of sight is often out of mind, getting them organized is often put off until they become a source of frustration and desperation.

BEDROOM ZONES

Basic organizing principles apply in the bedroom just as anywhere else. Creating zones for the activities allows for a functional placement of the items. Using them becomes more efficient and easier to maintain. There can be several zones in a bedroom depending on the size of the room and other spaces in the home, etc. I have listed some of them here, but you may have other zones that suit your home and lifestyle.

- ## Sleeping zone

     I assume the original purpose of a bedroom was to have a bed for sleeping since it is so named. A place to be able to rest and sleep is as significant to your health as exercise and nutrition. It is important to keep that area as clear as possible so sleep is not disturbed with things on the bed. Whatever it takes, do not leave anything on the bed while you sleep.

     Other items that might be included in a sleeping zone are a bedside table or chest that can hold a lamp for getting up in the middle of the night, a flashlight, tissues and a phone. For maximum organization and storage, choose a table with a drawer or shelf or choose a small chest with drawers.

- ## Leisure/Study zone

     For those who want a quiet place to read, study, listen to music or even watch television (God forbid but I am being real here), creating a space for that is important. If the space is large enough to contain a comfortable chair, that is preferable to using the bed. It would be better for your back and neck and better for the wear on the bed.

     Include a table, small chest or shelf to hold supplies you will need including the books, remotes, CD player, pens, pencils and note pad in a convenient location.

     If space is limited, the chair could be placed near the bedside table or chest.

- ## Dressing zone

     Unless there is a large dressing room with an area for clothing storage, most bedrooms contain furniture and closets for clothing. To have the most efficient use of space, the bedroom should have a dressing zone. Clothing should be stored, put on and taken off in the dressing zone. This means any dressers, chests, hooks, hangers and closets should be arranged as close to each other as is possible within the space.

Install a full length mirror somewhere in the room so that you can check you appearance from head to toe before you leave the house.

CLOSETS

Closets prove the rule that stuff will fill any vacant space. Regardless of the size or configuration of the closet, the space in them is always filled with something.

The organizing principle of limiting items to the space that will contain them is very difficult to follow in clothing closets. We want so many clothes and we find ways to overfill the closets by cramming items in them.

CLOTHING LIMITS

This brings us back to the discussion of setting limits. Seriously considering exactly how many items in each category of clothing we actually need is an important first step in the organizing process of the closet. It will facilitate the decisions on which clothing items to keep or pass on and which items could be added in future purchases.

Before you look in your closet, dresser or chest, stop and think about how you spend your days and what you need to wear for each activity. Make a list of the types of clothing you need and how many of each.

If you wear suits to work, how many would you need? If you work out at the gym three times a week, what and how many outfits would you want? Going through this exercise will help you as you make the decisions on what you already have and what you will add to your wardrobe. Making a list for reference can help in those choices. Do it before you go any further in organizing your clothing. It will save time later on.

ORGANIZING CLOTHING

As the purging and sorting process begins, each piece of clothing should be evaluated. Look over each piece of clothing carefully, try it on if necessary and apply these statements to it.

- If it no longer fits or is uncomfortable to wear, it should be moved on.
- If it is out of style or not flattering, it should be moved on. Forget the idea of saving it because styles repeat themselves. When it does come back in style it will be different in length, color, etc. and not what you hoped it to be.
- If it needs repairing, it should be placed in that sorting category.
- If it needs cleaning, it should be placed in the laundry area or the car for the trip to the cleaners.
- If you have not worn it in a year but it fits you and your wardrobe, it may be passed on or put in the "I am not sure" category discussed earlier.
- If you like it and it fits but you don't have anything to go with it, consider making a list of coordinating items you would like to buy so that you can wear it.
- If you already have enough of that item, let the extras be moved on. (Go back to the list you made on how much of each type of clothing you need.)
- Is it worth the trouble it causes? Too much care, snagging easily, riding up or down on your body, catching on other items, etc. are all reasons to move clothes out of your closet and life.

It is thought that clothing belongs to Pareto's 80/20 rule. Applied here it means 80% of the time you choose to wear only 20% of the clothes you own. More than likely you repeatedly wear the clothing that is the most comfortable, looks the best on you and is the most versatile with your lifestyle and other items in your closet. Look through your clothing and determine if that is true for you. Those are the pieces you want to keep and use to guide you as you build a wardrobe.

If you have established a limit for how many pieces of clothing in each category you need, then deciding which items to keep is easier for you. When every piece has been evaluated and sorted, then you are ready to organize your closet.

CLOSET CONFIGURATIONS

If it is possible to have all of your clothing removed from the closet, then deciding how the pieces should be placed in it is much easier. If you wear mostly separates, you may want to consider having two levels of hanging rods for those. If dresses are a large part of your wardrobe or if you prefer hanging slacks with clips attached to the waistband, then providing sufficient hanging room for them is important.

Some closets can be configured to have different levels of rods arranged in them by inserting a hanging rod that can be dropped from a current rod to create more hanging space. Hanging shelves, shoe racks and specialty hangers can also be included if needed.

Some rod and shelf systems are designed so they are adjustable. Components are attached to bars which have adjustable slots for attaching the shelf or rod. If you are considering a complete make over for the closet, then you will need to take measurements after your clothing choices are made.

Many do it yourself products are available or you can hire specialist to do it for you. There are closet companies that can create a custom system and specific design for your needs. If you choose to do it yourself, be sure to measure the width and length of the clothing as well as the size of the closet spaces as well as your clothing.

When the closet is configured like you want it, then replacing the clothing in an organized arrangement is important. Personal preference is the most important consideration since your selection of clothing each day is a personal choice.

Closet Doors

In addition to rod or shelf configurations, you can add storage to a closet by replacing sliding doors with bi-fold or swinging doors. This will enable you to see both sides of the inside of the closet at once. You can also use the inside of the door for hanging hooks and racks for extra storage and organization.

Organizing by Color

You may prefer grouping your clothing by color so that you can mix and match the items in an outfit. In this system all items of the same color would be placed together. Since the same color of pants, dresses, tops and jackets would be arranged together, this arrangement does not utilize the space as efficiently as other systems.

Organizing by Ensemble

If you have purchased or created complete ensembles or outfits, then you may want to place those together in one section of the closet. This system makes getting dressed much quicker since the planning of what items go together is already done. Depending on how many outfits you create, they may only need part of the space in the closet and the remaining space can be organized differently.

Organizing by Clothing Type

Organizing all pants together, all tops together, etc. is the most efficient use of space in the closet. Because they all fit within a common space, other items can be arranged around them.

It is possible to also arrange by color with those types which allows more versatility in creating outfits but may take more time getting dressed as you have to choose what to put together. An example would be red tops together, and then white tops, then blue tops, etc. all arranged in order together on the same rod.

When clothing is arranged this way you may see that you have more items in one type and color than you actually need. If you have 10 blue tops and you only need 3 then it is time to move out the extras.

Rotation Systems

Within those systems, you may choose to rotate the clothing so items are worn evenly. One client wore suits, dress shirts and ties to work everyday. His suits were arranged together on the rod and each morning he would pull out the suit at the front of the group to wear. When he changed clothes after work, he placed that suit at the back of the group. This could be done with other types of clothing but may be more difficult if clothing is also sorted by colors.

A rotation system is also good for determining which clothing you wear most and which are not worn at all. After you wear an item, put it at the front of that group. At the end of the season, you may find items at the back of the group that were never worn. These can be donated.

Another option is to begin the closet organization with all clothing hung so the hanger hook is placed on the rod from the back and the open part of the hook faces outward. After a garment is worn, it can be replaced on the rod as hangers are normally hung with the hook facing the back of the closet.

If some hooks are still facing outward at the end of a season, then these garments have not been worn and should be donated.

GARMENT HANGERS

My recommendations for hangers are based on trial and error of many types both at retail shops and online. Each closet and types of garments are different and the solutions can vary because of that. Without seeing the specific situation, I can only give you my overall recommendations based on organizing many closets for many years.

- ## Wooden, Shaped Shoulders

    If you have unlimited resources and very large closets, I recommend the wooden variety that have the sloping shoulder with the greatest angle to prevent dimples, have swivel hooks and are at least 1" wide and rounded at the ends. They are found at specialty shops such as Bed, Bath and Beyond or The Container Store and run $5-$10 for each hanger.

    While they are the best for the garments, easy to use and give a uniform appearance to the closet, their expense and the amount of space they take in the closet make them less practical for most of us for all garments. I recommend you look at them in order to make comparisons to other types of hangers. These are the best of the best and are the preferred choice for heavier garments such as coats and suits. This is the type that is used in most televised closet make over programs.

- ## Other Wooden Hangers

    Less expensive wooden hangers should be used for slacks and coats. Because they are sturdy and do not bend under the weight of heavier clothing, they are recommended for those items. They are not necessarily any better for lighter weight tops or shirts, and they may cost more than other choices that would be good for keeping the closet and the remainder of your clothing in order.

- ## Non-Slip Plastic Tubular

Except for special garments, I recommend the non-slip plastic tubular suit or dress hangers. They are carried by Wal Mart under the Mainstays brand and are called Non-Slip Suit Hangers. They are less expensive than the best wooden varieties and usually come in a package of 5.

When you see them you will notice they have gripper strips to keep clothes (including pants) from falling off without grabbing them like the flocked or felted metal hangers, have hooks for thin straps, have a nice slope to prevent shoulder dimples and have a swivel hanging hook for easier hanging. They are the sturdiest of the plastic hangers I have found, are easy to find in the store or online and can be used with other plastic hangers for a uniform look in the closet.

- ## Heavy Plastic Tubular

My next recommendation would be one of the heavier plastic tubular hangers that are usually sold in packages of 5 or 10. Be sure to look for the heavier types as the thinner ones will eventually bend. They have good slope and support for most garments and are the best buy, but they do allow some garments to slip off. One color will give a more uniform look but I have had clients that color coded them with the types of garments.

- ## Specialty Hangers

If there is room in the closet or on the back of the closet door, purchasing specialty hangers can help organize the space. There are many sizes and shapes of hanging shelves that can be hung on the closet rod. Some are designed for shoes but can contain purses, rolled underwear or T-shirts or socks. Larger shelf units can hold sweaters, T-shirts, underwear, etc. There are also hangers for jewelry, caps, belts, etc.

- ## Least Recommended

One thing to remember is that clothes by their very construction take up a certain amount of space so having super thin hangers will only make more space in your closet if you push your garments together, wrinkling and distorting their shape. Flocked or velvet covered thin metal hangers are compact only with thin or slinky clothing but not with normal items. They also do not release the garments easily so taking your clothing off of them can be a hassle. Some have been known to shed their fuzz onto the garments.

While padded hangers create great space for garments, they do not prevent dimples in clothing because they do not have enough shoulder slope, they are more expensive and they take up more space on the closet rod.

The cascading or multiple garments per hanger type are my least favorite but in some cases it may be the only choice. I have used them in older homes and college dormitories where the tiny closets would not hold the clothing any other way. Garments are very difficult to hang or remove from them when more than one item is already on them. They must be pulled out of the closet in order to use them and require awkward handling to place and remove the clothing. They do allow for more garments to be hung in a small space so they may be preferred in very small closets or hanging spaces.

OTHER CLOSET SPACES

Shelves

If garments are stacked on closet shelves, vertical dividers can be purchased that clip onto the shelf and these spacers will separate one stack from another. This prevents the stacked items from falling over and allows you to remove items from one stack without disturbing the items in adjoining stacks.

Shoes

The floor space in closets is often the dumping ground for shoes and other miscellaneous items. If at all possible keep the floor space empty. If shoes are kept there, they should be placed in a rack or shelves designed for them. Depending on how close the hanging garments are to the floor will determine how the shoes will be placed. Other options for shoes are placing them in hanging shoe bags with small shelf type compartments. These keep the shoes clean and are visible for easy access.

Shoes can be kept in boxes and placed on the shelf or floor if space allows. Do not stack more than 2 together as pulling out the bottom box will be more difficult. Use the clear plastic boxes or place a picture of the shoes or a descriptive label at the end of the box.

OTHER SHELVES AND DRAWERS

Whenever possible, shelves and drawers in chests or cabinets for additional clothing should be located close to the closet for convenience in dressing. Garments in this furniture is sorted and organized with the same process as in the closet.

- Purge any items that are not worn, that do not fit or that need repair. Do not save items for a special occasion someday. They are taking valuable space. Keep only those garments that you actually use.

- Use dividers and/or containers within the drawers and shelves. Some specialty containers are available for separating all types of clothing including socks, bras, lingerie and more. You could use simple boxes to do the same thing. Before making any purchases be sure to measure the spaces.

- Rather than stacking similar clothing in a drawer, some items can be rolled and arranged so that each piece is visible. This keeps you from having to dig under piles to get what you need. On shelves, rolled items can be placed upright in containers which go on the shelf.

Dream Drawer Dividers

Jewelry and Accessories

Adding accessories to an outfit is like putting frosting on a cake. It makes the ensemble better. There is no one perfect way to store them but they should be purged and sorted just as you have the other items.

- Keep only the items you are currently using and coordinate with the garments you now have.

- Keep like items together and containerize them.
- Throw away the little boxes that held the jewelry when purchased.
- Shoe bags with pockets hanging across the front are good choices for scarves, gloves and large pieces of jewelry.
- Similar bags with smaller pockets are available for smaller jewelry, hair bows and clips and ornaments.
- Peg racks and other hooks can be used for necklaces, belts and ties.
- Shallow drawers can be used for jewelry that is placed in divided containers. These can be stacked if space allows.
- Specialty containers with varying sizes of compartments can be purchased and placed on dresser tops or in drawers. Be sure to measure and count the number of compartments you need.
- The hidden space behind the entry door to the bedroom can be used to hang accessory items on racks.
- Consider limiting your earrings to one pair of gold or silver posts or small hoops. Better yet, invest in a pair of pearl posts. These choices go with any other accessories and outfits and make getting dressed so much faster and storage much simpler.

MORE BEDROOM AND CLOTHING TIPS

- Keep an open hamper in every bedroom to prevent clothing from being dropped on the floor.
- Store off season clothing at the back of the closet or under the bed in closed containers. The Ziploc Flexible Tote is perfect for this. Purchase bed lifts if necessary.
- Keep the number of empty hangers in a closet to a minimum. Store extras in the laundry or other storage areas.

- Keep items off the floor. Only furniture and rugs should be allowed to remain on it.

- Use trays, baskets or other decorative containers for small items on dressers, chests and tables. Keep these to a minimum.

- Place your alarm clock across the room so you have to get out of bed to turn it off. This will help get you up and moving.

- Pass on orphan clothing that has lost some of its components.

- Consider using shelves over windows for family pictures or other collectibles.

- Keep a list of clothing items you need to purchase to complete an outfit or to replace those that are worn or in disrepair.

- Bed linens can be stored in a separate linen closet or in the bedroom. Store blankets and pillows on top shelves in the closet.

- Sheets can be folded together with pillowcases and placed in the closet or between the mattress and springs. Unlike the princess and the pea, you will not even know they are there.

Chapter 13

CHILDREN'S ROOMS

hildren's rooms are a unique challenge to keep organized because they outgrow their furniture, clothing and toys about the same time as you have figured out how to keep them in order.

Then there is the abundance of items now available to keep your babies and children well fed, clothed and entertained. When I was a professional educator I was amazed at the so called educational toys, videos, games, etc. that were out there luring unsuspecting parents into the overindulgence trap.

We all have seen the child who chooses to play in the cardboard box that held the riding horse or life size train engine. That should give us a clue into what children need.

ORGANIZING PRINCIPLES

Any organizing plan will be most successful when you give children:

- Specific limits on literally everything but love and affection.
- Structure, routines and boundaries that make them feel safe and secure
- A good example and role model as you exercise organizing strategies

ZONES

Children's rooms should be arranged in zones for the uses and activities of that space. Most of those rooms have the following zones.

Sleeping Zone

- A crib, youth bed or standard bed is needed depending on the age of the child. The child outgrows the crib usually in 2-3 years or as soon as he learns to climb out of it. Some of those can convert into a youth bed which is a good choice if you are willing to stick to it and not purchase another youth bed in the shape of a race car, train or princess castle.

- Single or twin beds are usually the next step for sleeping. If children share a room with siblings, the bunk or trundle style saves space in the room. Adding a bed rail to keep the child from falling out is an option as well as a night light for middle of the night trips to the bathroom.

- The sleeping zone should also include simple or no bedding supplies. It is recommended you put no blankets, pillows, etc. in bed with an infant. As the child gets older, a simple sheet and blanket can be added and possibly a pillow.

- Resist the option of filling the bed with stuffed animals.

- Teach the child how to pull up the covers and/or make the bed as soon as he is able to get out of it by himself.

Dressing Zone

- An infant may have more clothes than he can wear before he outgrows them, so it is a good idea to save tags and receipts. Most of their clothing items can fit in a changing table or small chest.

- Children's furniture should have as much versatility as possible. Some chests now have tops that will hold pads for changing and can be later used as simple chests. Some dressing tables can later function in the laundry or craft area. If the furniture will be used for more than one child, try to make use of it in the child's room until the next one arrives. Try to think ahead for possible future uses before making the purchases.

- Standard closets are not child friendly. Systems should be put at their level so they can be responsible for the care of their things. Get down on their level to see the space as they see it.

- Rods for hanging clothes should be lowered or a lower one added so the child can reach it. Hooks, peg racks and hanging organizing racks and bags can be added to help the child get and put away his things. Pockets in shoe bags can hold small toys, as well as mittens, socks, hair bows, etc.

- Any drawers used for clothing should be labeled with pictures to help a young child find and return their things. Shallow drawers are preferable to stacking clothing. Plastic stacking drawers are ideal for young children as they are lightweight and easy to pull out and push in.

- An open clothes hamper should be placed in the closet or room so the child will be encouraged not to put clothes on the floor. When you have folded the clean clothes, return them to the room in a laundry basket and allow the child to put them away in the proper containers. Older children can fold their own clothing.

- Off season clothing or larger clothing passed on for later use can be stored in containers on higher shelves. Clothing that has been outgrown can be boxed for younger siblings or to pass on. All containers should be labeled with the size, sex and season for good identification.

Play Zone

Unless you have a playroom or section of the living space designated for toys, there should be an area in the child's room for play.

- Children learn from their toys but there should be limits on how many they own and how many they can have out at one time. Decide what that will be ahead of time and stick to it. Encourage relatives and friends to give clutter free gifts to your children.

- Toys should be more difficult to get out than put away. Books that are stored upright on a shelf are easy to pull out and more difficult to put back in order. A better choice would be a dishpan, bucket or basket that makes the child look for the book he wants but will be easy for him to drop it back in when he is done with it.

- Depending on the age of the child, most toys should be kept in open bins arranged in cubes or shelves and labeled so that clean up easy. Picture labels can be used for toddlers and large word labels for children learning to read.

- Some special toys or games can be stored on a higher shelf where only a parent can reach it as a reward or incentive for cooperation, responsibility, etc.

- Hanging pockets and plastic stacking drawers are good choices for small toys such as doll clothes, matchbox cars or train pieces.

- Puzzles should be kept in their original box. The corners may need to be reinforced with clear tape. Another choice is zip lock bags with the picture included. Color code the backs of the pieces for each puzzle with markers or crayons. Then the correct pieces can be returned to the proper box if more than one puzzle is out at a time.

- Other storage options are over the window shelving to display some collectible toys, corner nets to hold stuffed animals and totes on wheels to transport toys that can be taken to other rooms temporarily.

Study/Project Zone

Depending on the age of the child a table, desk or work surface is a good idea to include in their room.

- A table with adjustable legs is a cost effective way to provide a work surface for many years. Appropriate chairs should be added to it.
- Provide a tack strip or cork board for displaying the child's work. Any work to be saved can be included in the memory box described in the paper organizing Chapter 11.
- Older children will need furnishings for study materials and homework. Wall shelves for books and drawers for desk supplies may be needed as well.

MAINTAINING THE SPACE

Consistency and vigilance are the names of the maintenance game for children. Some hints to keep you on track are given here but you will need to develop your own standards and routines.

- Use the change of seasons to purge clothing and toys. This is the time to teach your children organizing strategies and the importance of sharing and giving. Let them participate in the process.
- Apply the one in one out rule with toys. Set a limit as to how many different things your children can have and stick to it. It will cause them to develop decision making skills as they have to choose which to let go.

- Take pictures of you child with their toys before donating them.

- Discard and do not donate broken toys or clothing in disrepair. Do not give away anything you would not want given to your child.

- If toys will be saved for younger children, box them up and label them for storage elsewhere.

- Use under the bed storage for items used less often.

- Require children to put their toys away after using them. Allow only one or two toys out at a time.

- Set a time limit for toy clean up. Set a timer or require it before a treat, a trip out, television, video, computer time, or a snack. Be specific with what you want done not just a general clean up request.

- Toys left out should go into a donate box. They may be claimed after a chore is done. If it is not claimed in a week, it is donated.

- Begin the chore routine as soon as the child can walk. Simple requests such as "Put the doggie in the box." can be done by a toddler.

- Don't do anything for the child that he can do for himself. It will build his self confidence and independence. After all you want him to grow up to be able to live on his own, right? It is never too early to think ahead.

- Before children leave a room, they should put away their toys. This includes when your children visit in the homes of other children. Ten minutes before you leave, have your child help the host child clean the space even if it was not so tidy when you arrived. Be a good guest and set an example for when other children come to your house. You may need to give guidance or help with directions in putting the toys away, and you should insist that all the children participate.

Chapter 14

KITCHENS

for most families the purchase of a home involves a careful look at the kitchen. It is not only the place where meals are prepared but also where some meals are eaten and family members gather to socialize. More contemporary homes are designed with an open kitchen to the dining and family living areas. Some kitchens are smaller but they can be organized with the same principles. It is important to make this space as efficient and attractive as possible.

KITCHEN ORGANIZING PRINCIPLES

- Strive to maintain clear counters. Store as few items as possible on them.
- Provide adequate containers for storing items. Group similar items together.
- Measure spaces when they are emptied for future reference in purchasing organizing products.
- Place items used most often closest to where they are used.
- Commit to finding and maintaining a permanent home for each item.

- Review the questions to ask about keeping items in Chapter 8. Kitchens are infamous for harboring clutter. Be ruthless in getting rid of gadgets and appliances, etc. that have little or no use.

ZONES

Kitchens are normally zoned around the sink as a cleaning zone, the range as a cooking zone and the refrigerator as the food storage zone. If a pantry is located in the kitchen, it would be in the food storage zone also. For organizing purposes, I have simplified these zones since some areas overlap.

Food Preparation, Cooking and Storage

- Arrange food items, cookware and utensils used in food preparation as close to the range and refrigerator as possible.
- Remove items from one cabinet at a time and sort.
- Dispose of any expired food products, broken appliances, containers without lids, lids without containers and excess margarine tubs, grocery bags, etc. that you may have collected.
- Place any food products, cookware, appliances or utensils you do not use in a donate or sell container.
- Clean the cabinet and place a shelf liner that can be wiped clean on the shelf.
- Place similar types of food items together.
- Canned foods can be placed on stair step shelves that can adjust to the width of the cabinet, in gravity feed containers like those used for soda cans or on pull out shelves or racks.
- Spices can be stored on smaller stair step shelves in cabinets or drawers or on turntables.

- Boxes of cereals, pastas, rice and other dry goods that have been opened should have the contents moved to air tight containers. Clear plastic containers or recycled clear glass food containers with labels are good choices.

- Use a standard size of food container for leftovers. The lids should fit the shallow and deeper containers to make organizing easier. Square and rectangular containers use space more efficiently and clear containers make identification easier.

- Free standing wire shelves, under the shelf wire baskets, pull out wire baskets or shelves and turntables are all options to add more storage space in the cabinets.

- Drawer dividers should be used to contain utensils, knives and other small items.

- Potholders should be kept near the range in a drawer or container on the counter.

- Hanging racks with hooks from the ceiling or placing a towel rod or dowel with hooks on the wall under cabinets can be used for pots and pans or large utensils.

- Magnetic tool strips can be mounted on the wall for knives and other metal utensils.

- Racks and hooks can be placed inside cabinet doors to hold smaller items.

- Pull out shelves and/or wire baskets are essential for storing items in the back of lower base cabinets. It is very difficult to reach items so near the floor and so far inside the cabinet.

- Store small packets of drink mix or sauce and seasoning mixes together in small square containers on the shelf.

- Wire racks designed to hold pan lids can be used in deep cabinets to store cookie sheets and baking pans vertically rather than stacking them. Cabinets over built in ovens are an ideal placement for these. Permanent vertical dividers are also a good idea for that space.

- Pot lids can be hung inside some cabinet doors on specialty racks or behind a towel bar mounted so the handle at the top of the lid catches on the rod.

- Label shelves inside cabinets so that other family members will return items to their home.

- If your pantry or refrigerator has wire shelves, consider purchasing acrylic or plastic shelf covers. Measure for a good fit.

- The refrigerator should have similar items grouped together.

- Use the designated bins in refrigerators for those items. They are designed to maintain the correct temperature and humidity for those items.

- Add turntables, free standing wire shelves and other space saving items to the refrigerator to keep items organized.

- The door is the warmest part of the refrigerator. Do not store eggs, milk or meats in it for food safety reasons.

- Cookbooks should be stored near this zone, but should be purged so that they do not take up valuable space. Try not to store any on the counters.

- Cookbooks you do not use can be donated or sold. If you must keep those, consider displaying them on the hidden spaces at the tops of counters or on shelves over doors or windows in the kitchen.

- Keep an attractive container with pens, pencils, note pad and scissors in a convenient location in case they are needed.

- Loose recipes can be placed in plastic page protectors in the household notebook, other type notebook or in card files.

- Consider storing favorite recipes on computer files and using the Internet sources for finding new recipes. This will cut out the need for cooking magazines and clipping recipes. If there is a food product you want to make, there is more than one recipe for it online. My favorite web sites are listed in the resources section.

Serving and Cleaning Zone

- Cleaning products should be stored under or near the sink unless there are small children in the house. Even childproof locking systems can be undone by clever toddlers so care should be taken to keep any hazardous substances out of their reach.

- Under the sink is a difficult storage area because of plumbing and the depth of the cabinet and its closeness to the floor. Special pull out wire and plastic baskets are available to install on the floor of the cabinet that will fit around plumbing. Using those or other containers for supplies that can be pulled forward is the best use of that space.

- Eliminate any cleaning products not used, extra dish cloths or towels or those too worn to be used again.

- Dishcloths and dishtowels can be rolled and placed in drawers or upright in containers that sit on a shelf. This is preferable to a stack that can fall over.

- Sort dinnerware as it is removed from the cabinet and be ruthless in deciding what to keep. Souvenir mugs, odds and ends of dinnerware sets and items never used should be removed and donated or sold. If Grandma's china is there and it has never been used, see if a family member wants it.

- Ideally the dinnerware, flatware and serving pieces are near the sink and/or dishwasher so that once they are cleaned, they can quickly be put away. The next best storage for them is near the area where the family eats so that serving is facilitated.

- Adding free standing wire shelves will make storing dinnerware and glasses easier in tall cabinets. Stacking different size items such as saucers on dinner plates is not practical or preferred.

- Hooks can be installed on the underside of shelves for hanging cups if there is space above other items below. Similar rails are available for hanging stemware.

- Under the shelf racks for holding placemats or other linens can be hooked over the front edge of shelves to give additional storage space.

- Store flatware in rectangular containers rather than those with molded shapes for each piece. Individual containers for each size of flatware are preferable to large containers with sections that may not adapt to many sizes of drawers.

- Place a washable mat in front of the sink to absorb drips and prevent slipping.

- Store special occasion and less frequently used items in the hard to reach shelve or in another storage space in the house. Save the convenient spaces for items you use everyday.

MAINTENANCE

Keeping the kitchen cleaned is a constant battle because it is used so often and such a mess is made each time a meal is prepared or eaten.

- Try to clear and clean the counters after each meal.
- Keep the cleaning supplies close to the sink so they are easily reached.
- Clean the floor at least once a day. Dirt and hidden food can be trapped in the smallest crevice.
- Use dish cloths rather than sponges as they can be more thoroughly cleaned for sanitation purposes.

- Use dish towels rather than paper towels as they are more earth friendly and economical.

- Allow children to take part in kitchen chores. Even pre-school children can take their plate and utensils to the sink when they have been excused from the table. Older children can set the table, unload the dishwasher and take out the trash.

- Make meal time a pleasant occasion. It is not the time to discuss serious or negative topics. This is a place to make good memories.

Chapter 15

BATHROOMS

homes today are being built with more than one bathroom and even older homes that are being renovated include another bathroom. It is one of the remodeling projects that gives more value than it costs. Since they are normally smaller spaces with lots of fixtures, keeping them orderly is important.

Regardless of how many bathrooms you have, the same organizing principles apply. I am assuming they are being used by more than one person and that some of the time used in getting dressed is spent there.

BATHROOM ORGANIZING PRINCIPLES

- Keep the sink and counter as clear as possible, Contain any items that must be placed there.
- Keep bathroom supplies close to where you use them.
- Use containers to hold similar type items. Clear plastic is best.
- Label all containers for convenience and safety. This is critical with medicines, drugs and toiletries.

- Purge items often. Dispose of expired or old products and store duplicates elsewhere.
- Create a realistic but emphatic maintenance routine with family members.

BATHROOM ZONES

Although bathrooms are small spaces they have a lot going on in them. Each of those activities has fixtures and supplies creating zones.

Bathing Zone

- The bathtub and/or shower should have a container for holding soap, shampoo, etc. One made of wire with or without plastic coating is preferable since it drains completely and needs cleaning less often. Multi level containers should be used for children to be able to reach the items. Try not to use the ledges of the fixture for products.
- Towel bars should be located near the area so it can be easily accessed after bathing.
- Hooks for hanging towels is easier for children to use. These should be place low enough for the children to reach them.
- Consider assigning towel colors or designs to each member of the family. This can prevent many arguments over what belongs to whom. Small children love character towels and even teenagers will accept them in their favorite color.
- Towels can be rolled and stored in containers. This eliminates stacks of towels from falling over or a mess created when the towel at the bottom of a stack is wanted.
- Towels can be rolled together with wash cloths and hand towels if that is the way they are used. If not, use separate containers for each of them.

- Towels can be stored on shelves or in cabinets in the bathroom depending on the space available. Personal towels can be kept in the bedroom on a shelf or in a drawer. A towel bar for hanging them on the back of the door can be used in each bedroom. Linen closets are another option.

- If there is room, a hamper for towels, underwear, etc. is a good idea.

Regent Tension Pole Shower Caddy

Toilet Zone

- Extra toilet paper and other necessities should be stored close to the fixture. Vertical paper holders are available that take less floor space and hold several rolls. If you purchase toilet paper in bulk, store additional rolls elsewhere.

- If funds and décor allow it, purchasing a toilet paper holder that has an open arm roller rather than the spring loaded type is a great investment for convenience and sanity. Whoever designed the spring type most of us own should have been hung at sun down. I am sure I am not the only one to drop part or all of it in the toilet as it shot out of my hands within 2 seconds of being taken off the holder. In fact, there has rarely been a time that I could hold one together the entire time I was replacing the roll of paper.

- A shelf, rack or basket can be used to hold small items, notepad and pencil and reading material for those who might want them.

Dressing Zone

- Most of the time spent in the bathroom is preparing oneself for entering the world that will see us. This is around the sink. Keep it and the counter as clear as possible.

- Use attractive trays, baskets or other containers to hold items that must be kept on the counter. Toothbrushes and hairbrushes can be placed vertically in attractive cups. Lotions, powders and creams can be positioned on trays.

- Each person using the space should have their own drawer or container for their personal supplies. If there is no room in the bathroom, the containers can be stored in the bedroom and carried in and out as needed. If there is room in cabinets, shelves or drawers for them, they should be labeled with the person's name.

- If drawers are deep, stacking divided trays can be used for small items. These are available in container and bath supply stores.

- Store duplicates of items off site in another storage area. Use the older product first.

- If large containers of shampoo and other products are purchased in bulk, refill smaller containers with the product and store the larger one elsewhere.

- Travel size products may be inserted in a first aid kit or travel bag. Additional items should be donated.

- Cosmetics that have expired should be disposed. Most only last a few months and mascara less than that. Some suggest changing it with the seasons. Purge any that you no longer use.

- A magnifying mirror attached to the wall is a better choice than a portable one unless you have a vanity for dressing. It saves space and is convenient.

- Place towel bars or hooks near the sink for hanging hand towels and wash cloths.

- Additional storage can be added with shelves or cabinets over the toilet, skirts around free standing sinks or hanging shoe bags on the back of the door. Each row of the shoe bag could be given to a different person for their items.

- Pull out shelves and wire or plastic baskets are available to insert under the sink. They are designed to go around plumbing and allow items to be stored in the back of the cabinet with easy access.

- Single and double level turntables and free standing wire shelves can be used in cabinets and on shelves to give more organized storage space.

MAINTENANCE

Clean up for the bathroom is important for sanitation and organization. Chore charts for it can be made just as in the kitchen.

- Waterproof shelf liners should be placed in all drawers and shelves.

- If space permits, keep a container with cleaning supplies in the bathroom.

- Consider dark towels or disposable cloths for removing make up.

- Expired medicines should be flushed down the toilet or garbage disposal. Do not throw them away in a waste basket where children, pets or others could find them.

- Keep floors as dry as possible with washable rugs. Falls can happen from slipping on wet floors.

- Use spray on shower cleaners for daily tub and shower cleaning. They will prevent soap scum from hardening on the fixtures.

- Install ventilation fans if they are not already there to keep mildew from forming so quickly.

Chapter 16

FAMILY AND LIVING SPACES

1iving rooms, family rooms or dens are gathering places for the family and many different types of activities take place in them. Clutter can become like background wallpaper because we get so used to seeing it there. Many items find their homes on the floor which makes cleaning more difficult. It might be necessary to involve all the family members in creating the organizational plan for this room.

FAMILY ROOM ORGANIZATIONAL PRINCIPLES

- Be willing to purge items no longer used or needed to open up the space.
- Place items close to where they are used and within reach of all family members.
- Use containers on surfaces and in cabinets, shelves and drawers to hold similar items.
- Place labels on shelves and containers so they are easily seen.

- Group collections of items together.

- Use hidden areas over windows and doors, under sofas, and in functional furniture.

- Keep as many items as possible off the floor to make clean up easier and the room appear more spacious.

ZONES

Since so many activities take place in the family room much of the furniture will serve multiple purposes. Zones will overlap but specific items should be within easy reach for each activity.

Entertainment

- Arrange electronic items such as televisions, CD and DVD players and video games in one area so the wires and cables can be contained together.

- Label each end of cables and wires related to the computer and other electronic equipment. It will save much time in connecting or reconnecting

- Use wire baskets that can be mounted under shelves or cable ties to contain wires.

- Purge videos, CDs and DVDs that are no longer used. Sell or donate them to a local charity, nursing home or hospital. If you want to locate one again they can be rented or borrowed from local libraries.

- Renting or borrowing movies and games is an excellent organizational choice and sets a good example for your children in managing finances and spaces.

- Store CDs and DVDs in their case vertically on shallow shelves or if space is limited, they can be removed from the case and placed in notebooks or cases with plastic sleeves. Sort and arrange by category.

- Videos can be stored vertically on shelves or in shoe box type containers. Do not stack flat as accessing those on the bottom is more difficult.

- Remotes and game joysticks should be contained in a basket, decorative box or container designed specifically for them. Keep them within easy reach of the chair or sofa.

- Place a table or shelf near every seating area. Large coffee tables can take the place of several small end tables. Choose one with storage shelves, cabinet doors or drawers. Provide an area for playing with toys if you will allow that activity. A lower cabinet can be used to store those items or they can be taken back to the bedroom in a tote box or rolling crate.

Overdoor elfa Media Rack

Reading and Leisure

- For reading areas be sure to have a comfortable chair with adequate lighting and a place to store books, magazines, newspapers, etc.

- Books should be purged from bookcases. Keeping fiction books that you have read serves no purpose except to prove you own them. Sell or donate them knowing you can borrow it from the library if you have time to read it again.

- Non-fiction books should be grouped by category. Since information is always changing, using older books as reference many not provide recent findings. Let them go and use the Internet to find the latest information. The books are not your brain and letting them go will not cause you to forget what you have learned. (Old age, however, may cause you to forget. I speak from experience once again.)

- Sets of encyclopedias are dated the moment you get them. Use the Internet or library for research. Use their encyclopedias if you want to teach your children how to use them.

- Make friends with the library. It is a wonderful place of knowledge and entertainment for your children and prevents book clutter from residing in your house. Most offer excellent programs for adults and children.

- Mix books, plants, attractive storage containers or photographs on bookshelves for more interesting arrangements.

- Use vertical areas to provide extra shelves or cabinets for storage.

- Upper bookcase shelves and over the window shelving can be used to display collectables and photographs.

- Collections of similar items are more attractive when grouped together in displays.

- Keep an attractive container with pens, pencils, note pad and scissors in a convenient location in case they are needed.

- Card tables can be used for board games, craft activities or other projects. When you are finished it can be folded and stored under the sofa, behind large furniture or in a nearby closet.

- If the family office is located in this room, reserve a space for a table or desk. A drawer or attractive containers can hold desk supplies. More about home offices is in Chapter 21.

- If a computer will be located in this room, consider placing a wireless system in your home to eliminate having to connect all of the components with cables.

MAINTENANCE

- Cover the surfaces with washable fabrics to cut down on dusting and polishing.

- Maintain a chore chart for vacuuming, dusting, etc.

- Require all game parts to be put away after use.

- Dispose of old magazines and newspapers. When the new issues come in, older issues should be donated. Be sure to remove any identifying labels from them before donating.

Chapter 17

DINING ROOMS

ost homes have a separate dining room or dining area large enough for the family to sit together for a meal. Even if an eating bar is located in the kitchen, a separate area is usually found for a table and chairs and often other storage furniture.

DINING ROOM ORGANIZING PRINCIPLES

- Provide adequate space for getting to the table and moving in and out of chairs.
- Locate storage furniture so it does not hinder traffic around the table.
- Store similar most often used items together.
- Consider multiple uses for the space if the room is rarely used for meals.
- Use hidden spaces if storage areas are limited.

ZONES

Dining rooms obviously have an eating zone, but storage areas are needed and rooms that are not normally used for meals can be used for other activities.

Mealtime Zone

- Provide adequate seating for all those eating together. Folding chairs can be used and stored in a closet or other storage area afterwards. Wooden posts located on the wall of the garage can be used to hang them so they do not take up floor space.
- If remodeling, consider hardwood, attractive ceramic or vinyl floors for easy clean up.
- Cloth or paper napkins can be placed in an attractive basket, bowl or tray and serve as a centerpiece.
- Placemats are more versatile to use than tablecloths and can be left on the table as decorations or stacked in the center with a napkin basket.
- Dinnerware, flatware and serving pieces should be located in an area convenient to setting the table and replacing after clean up.

Storage Zone

- Furniture used for storage should fit the size of the room. Pieces that are too large will make mealtime difficult.
- Corner cabinets are a great use of space and if large enough can store many types of items.
- Special occasion dinnerware or silverware should be kept only if used or you have sufficient space for it.
- Purge dinnerware sets that are incomplete, those you do not like or have broken and chipped pieces.

- Do not store china or other dinnerware sets that are never used away in packed boxes. If they are sentimental pieces or family heirlooms, pass them on to a family member or someone who will use or display them. If they are respectable items, demonstrate that by enjoying them and not packing them away or out of sight.

- Table cloths can be stored in shallow drawers or hung over a dowel or hanger covered with the empty roll from wrapping paper or paper towels. Slit the roll on one side and slip it over the rod. Hang it in a closet. This will prevent additional wrinkles.

- Additional linens can be stored in the drawers or shelves of dining room furniture such as chests or buffets. You may also use a linen closet if one exists.

- Consider placing a clothing chest with drawers in the dining room if no longer needed for clothing. It is ideal for linens.

Additional Activities

- Use the dining table for craft projects or other art activities. Cover the table with a protective cloth, cutting board or plastic before using it.

- The table may be a good choice for homework if the room is good for studying. A tote with desk supplies may be used and then stored when the work is done.

- If the family needs home office space, reserving a corner of the dining room for that activity is a good use of space. Choose a table or desk that compliments the other furnishings. Some items can be stored in the furniture already there or in rolling carts and file trolleys that can be moved to a nearby closet when not in use. More details about home offices are in Chapter 21.

- If there is not space in the family room for board games and card playing, those items could be stored in the dining room for use on that table.

MAINTENANCE

- Keep the tops of buffets, chests and china cabinets clear and free of clutter.
- Do not allow the table to become a dumping ground for items entering the house.
- Keep the table attractive with a centerpiece and/or tablecloth.
- Use washable decorative fabrics on surfaces to reduce the amount of dusting.

Chapter 18

ENTRANCES

b e it large or small the entrance sets the tone for the house. It is the first place you see and first impressions do count. We will discuss front and back entrances since most families use both.

ENTRANCE ORGANIZING PRINCIPLES

- Keep similar items together.
- Provide containers for items coming and going.
- Arrange items for attractiveness and function.

ZONES

The two obvious zones are the back and front entrances. Within those several activities take place that require items and arrangements for good organization.

Unloading Zone

- Provide containers to drop off incoming papers as close to the entrance as possible. This may be the incoming paper box discussed in Chapter 11, a basket or other small container that will hold items until they can be sorted later that day.

- Provide a shelf, a small table or chest to place containers for small items, hats, gloves, etc. Cover it with a plain or decorative washable fabrics or small quilt to give a warm touch to the entrance and cut down on dusting and polishing.

- Place hooks, small pegs or containers for keys.

- If shoes are removed when entering, provide a basket, crate or box for them to be contained. Otherwise they will move around and get misplaced. This could also be in the garage or a closet at the front door.

- Provide hooks or pegs for children's coats, backpacks or book bags or other totes.

- If a closet is available, hanging shelves or open shoe bags can be used for hats, gloves and other small items.

- Use wooden or other sturdy hangers in coat closets.

- Add space above the top shelf in the closet with additional shelves or stacking containers.

Other Zone Tips

- Provide a container for items to go out the door as you leave. A box or basket for envelopes to be mailed, books to be returned, etc. will help remind you to pick them up as you leave.

- Place an umbrella stand near the door for rainy days.

- Outdoor mats will help clean shoes before entering the house.

- A washable rug near the door will help dry wet shoes and keep dirt from being carried further into the house.

- Attractive plants and decorative containers help beautify the space. If you have access to fresh flowers and enjoy arranging them, they are the best welcome into your home. A simple bunch in a mug or vase is all that is needed. You do not have to be a professional florist to make it attractive.

- Keep the front walk, steps and porch clean. Wash any glass at the front door. It gives a good first impression.

Chapter 19

GARAGE, ATTIC AND OTHER STORAGE

Storage is a big issue with most families and much of it ends up in the garage or attic. Organizing those spaces and providing adequate storage for items makes it easier to find what you need and keep those items maintained.

GARAGE, ATTIC AND STORAGE ORGANIZING PRINCIPLES

Although these areas are different, some basic principles for storage apply to both garages and attics. We will consider them together here and separately under zones.

- Store similar items together in containers that are waterproof and insect proof.
- Use labels on the fronts and backs of containers.

- Consider color coding containers for holiday decorations so they are easily found when needed. Colored tops or bins are available most often during the specific season.

- Purge all tools, supplies and equipment that you no longer use, that are broken or in disrepair, that have duplicates or have been replaced with other items.

GARAGE ZONES

Vehicles

- Your car is a more expensive purchase than anything else in the garage. Make room for it in the garage to protect and extend its life.

- Make a space for the car in the garage and mark the floor where it will be located. No other items should be allowed in that space.

- Mark how far you should pull in with a landmark or hang a flag or similar item above the windshield so you will hit it when you have pulled the correct distance forward.

- Children's riding toys should have a spot designated specifically for it with the child's name on the space.

Workshop

- Keep as many items as possible off the garage floor.

- Group tools and supplies for the workshop by type much like you see in hardware stores.

- If your garage walls are unfinished, boards can be attached between the studs to provide support for attaching hooks and other organizing items.

- Provide a workbench with a work surface sufficient for projects done there.
- If there is no space for a permanent workbench, a drop down table top on hinges or a folding table can be used.
- Peg boards can hold hand tools. Draw the shape of the tool in its space to find its home easily when replacing it.
- Magnetic strips can be placed on the wall over the workbench to hold knives and other tools.
- Use shelves above and in the workbench itself to store paint, electrical and plumbing supplies in containers. The portable tool box should be placed there also.
- Nails, screws, bolts, etc. can be placed in small jars and the lids screwed to the underside of a shelf over the workbench. They can be easily seen and removed. Label them with the size and type of item stored there.

Sporting Equipment

- Sporting equipment should be stored together and sorted by sport.
- Bicycles for older children and adults can be hung on racks designed for them.
- Helmets for all sports can be hung on pegs
- Large balls can be stored in mesh bags hung from the ceiling or wall. Rolling racks designed specifically for them can also be used.
- Small balls can be stored in narrow trays mounted on the wall.
- When children have outgrown the equipment, move it out to sell or donate.
- Camping gear should be stored together and on shelves or cabinets off the floor.

Ball & Bat Storage Rack

Garden and Lawn Storage

- Garden tools with long handles can be hung on racks designed specifically for them. Long nails and pegs can also be used to insert into the holes in handles for hanging.

- Small garden tools can be stored in totes or other containers for portability.

- Fertilizers and other chemicals for the lawn and garden should be stored in covered bins or tubs. This keeps them dry and safely out of reach.

- Lawn mowers and other yard equipment should be cleaned before locating in the garage. Smaller equipment can be hung on the wall.

- Bottles of insecticides, herbicides, etc. should be stored on higher shelves for safety.

Garden Accessory & Tool Rack

Other Items

- Shelving units with uniform storage containers are the most attractive arrangements. These are good for holiday storage bins.
- Bulk purchase items can be stored on shelving designed especially for them.
- Cleaning supplies not kept in the house can be located in cabinets or shelving units.
- Keep a container with pens, pencils, note pad and scissors in a convenient location for when they are needed.

Attic Zone

- The extreme heat or cold in an attic requires care in the storage of items that are affected by temperatures. Decorative candles, some plastics including soft plastics in dolls, photographs, video and audio tapes and fragile fabrics are items that should not be stored there.

- For convenience and safety, install floor boards over the ceiling joists and adequate lighting overhead.

- To prevent insect infestation of papers, fabrics, etc. store those items in plastic containers with tight fitting lids.

- Store containers with similar items together so they can be easily located.

- Labeling containers with contents listed makes it easier to locate specific items.

- Mapping locations of containers will make locating them easier.

- When there are many containers, number them and keep an inventory system in your files.

- Wood furniture should be covered with old blankets or sheets.

- Upholstered furniture should not be stored in attics.

Other Storage Tips

- Basements are not usually found in homes along the coasts in the southern part of our country because of the low water table. If you have one, basements are a good option for storage if the space has not been converted into other living spaces such as bedrooms, family rooms, etc. Follow the same guidelines as for garages and attics. Humidity and other moisture problems may require special care of some items stored there.

- Rented storage units are the least recommended option. The expense of keeping items in them quickly adds up to more than those items are worth. If it is necessary for you to have one because of an upcoming move, remodel or other significant and temporary situation, then this may be your only option. Containers placed there should have tight fitting lids as insects abound in neighboring units and being very opportunistic creatures, they will visit your site quickly. Clean everything before returning items to your home.

Chapter 20

LAUNDRY SPACES

L aundry is an ever present job waiting to be done. Taking care of it in an efficient and timely manner is the goal. Having good organizing products and a good system will make the task easier.

LAUNDRY SPACE ORGANIZING PRINCIPLES

- Maximize any space you have for doing the laundry by limiting its function to laundry related activities.
- Use shelves, hooks and racks to hold supplies and clothing.
- Don't do anything a family member can do for himself.
- If you are a working gal, set aside a specific day or two for laundry. Do not let it become an all consuming or daily activity.

ZONES

Laundry zones are based on the activities since many laundry spaces are simply a closet with the washer and dryer or a corner of the garage or basement.

Laundry In

- Put a clothes hamper in each room so that gathering laundry is a simpler task. If clothing is not in the hamper, it will not be washed. Stick with this rule to teach children responsibility and accountability.

- Provide enough underwear, etc. for several days so you do not have to do laundry so often.

- Keep the top of the washer and dryer clear if they are side by side. This is a good place to pre treat, sort and fold clothing if a table or counter is not available..

- Installing shelves or cabinets above the appliances will provide adequate storage for detergents and other laundry products.

- If storage cannot be placed above the appliances, consider narrow rolling shelves that are designed to go between the washer and dryer or on the outside of one of them. These units often have a high bar for hanging clothing temporarily.

- Store small bottles of spot removers, etc. together in containers for better organization. Guides for stain removal can be placed in the containers, posted on the inside of cabinet doors or hung on the wall if necessary.

- Sort clothes near the washer when you have all you plan to wash together. Use several laundry baskets to do this and keep the loads separate. You can color code these baskets if it helps separate clothing colors and types.

- The amount of clothing in each category will determine how many loads you will wash. Combine as many as possible to reduce the number of loads.

- If large enough, consider loads containing only one or two persons clothing. Of course you are free to run small loads if your machine has adjustable water levels and shorter cycles.

- Wash loads with clothing where wrinkling won't matter first. Underwear is good for this. If these items sit awhile before folding nothing is lost.

- Setting a timer to monitor the loads is a good idea if none exists on your machines.

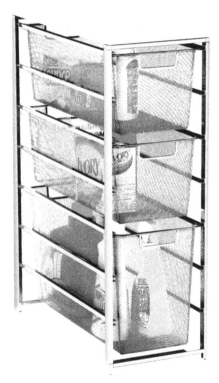

Platinum elfa Mesh Laundry Storage with Narrow Shelves

Laundry Out

- Remove items from the dryer as soon as possible. Sort items to be folded into laundry baskets labeled with the name of each person in the family.

- Items for hanging should be placed on hangers right away.

- If there is space, install a rod for hanging clothing. A tension shower rod will fit above the washer and dryer in some spaces. Closet dowels can also be cut to fit that space or other walls in the laundry area.

- If a door is available, an over the door rack for hanging clothing can be used.

- Rolling garment racks like used in clothing stores can be purchased at department stores if no other options are available. You want the clothing that will be hung in closets to leave that space on hangers.

- Fold the dry clothing as soon as possible. Use the top of your appliances or another flat surface.

- If you have no room for a counter or shelf suitable for folding, consider a folding table or carrying the basket to another space for folding.

- Let children who are old enough fold their own clothing. Leave the basket of clean clothing in their room.

- Folded clothing can be delivered to the room of each person in their basket. Even young children can put their folded clothing away if the drawers are labeled. They should return the baskets to the laundry room so you know the clothing has been put away. All of the baskets can be stacked together for storing and placed on the appliances if a shelf or floor space is not available.

Brushed Steel Garment Rack

Ironing Options

- Purchasing clothing that requires no ironing is the best organizing option. Items designed for traveling are the most suitable.

- Hang clothing immediately after drying to reduce the need for ironing.

- If space is available, consider installing an ironing board that stores on the wall or in a drawer. It can be folded away when not needed.

- Over the door and wall racks are available that will store the iron and ironing board until needed.

- Wrinkle release products can be purchased to spray on clothing so ironing is not needed.

Chapter 21

Hobbies, Collections and More

ur lives have become so full of activities that involve owning more things that need a place to be stored or used. Hobbies, collecting, special occasions and holidays all demand a space in our homes. Keeping them in order can be done.

Hobby Organizing Principles

Hobbies are a wonderful way to add dimension to our lives but can easily overtake our time and spaces. There are some good principles to follow to keep them organized regardless of which hobby you enjoy most.

- Limit the number of hobbies you take on: two is best or three if it is related to the one of the others. One client I have does scrap booking and knitting. She also does card making which involves many of the scrapbook supplies and tools.

- Do not try to purchase every new tool or supply for that craft when it comes along. Most specialty gadgets are rarely used and take up valuable space.

- Finish one project before you start another one. I know that is difficult when classes come along to teach a new technique. Go to the class and take notes if you must, but do not start another project. You will end up with more UFOs (unfinished objects) than FFOs (finally finished objects) and they will be a storage nightmare adding clutter to your space.

- Purchase kits when they are suitable. It will save you time in making choices and money in purchasing supplies you don't use.

- Use storage containers designed for your items if they are convenient for you to use. It is usually the most efficient use of space. If those are too expensive, try to find a less expensive but similar substitute container in the fishing tackle, laundry or kitchen storage area of the store.

- Some specialty storage items are difficult to use and take too much effort to get what you want out of them. Look for convenience in use for any storage solution. Think about where you will put it and how you will use it before you buy it. Trial and error can be expensive.

- Consider over the door style shoe bags with clear pockets for sorting and storing small items.

- Portable totes, rolling carts or drawers, wheeled suitcases and crates are all options when space is limited.

- Fill the closet in a spare room with shelving for containers or stackable drawers for your craft items.

- Folding or card tables can be used for projects if no other surfaces are suitable for your projects. These can be stored under beds, behind tall furniture or in other storage areas.

- Purge items you have not used and realize now you probably will never use. Our tastes and preferences change over time and there is no point in keeping something just because you thought you might use it. Sell or donate it to your craft group or guild.

- Store craft magazines and how to booklets in a magazine holder. When it is filled, use the one in one out principle.

- Provide adequate lighting for the project area.

- Label all containers.

- Use peg boards to store tools and supplies that are used often.

- Convert chests, china cabinets and other furniture into attractive storage for your supplies.

- If you are using supplies that could hurt little ones or pets, consider working on projects when they are not around.

- Clean up your mess before you leave it overnight or longer.

- Share your talents with groups or guilds and give handmade gifts to family and friends.

- If you are unhappy with your project results, give it to the first person who compliments it. They will be happy and you will be free of it as a reminder of your disappointment.

Jumbo Utility Cart

Photographs and Scrapbooks

- Begin with the current photos and work backwards.

- Discard unflattering, foggy or distorted photos.

- Be selective in those you save. Use the remaining good photos and duplicates in greeting cards or to decorate bags and other items.

- Invest in a digital camera and begin using online services to create scrapbooks, calendars, cards and more.

- Consider scanning older quality photos rather than saving them for scrapbooks. Companies that offer those services are listed in the resource section.

- Plan a photo give away day for those photos you no longer need or want. Spread them on a large surface or table and invite family to take what they want. Store the remaining photos no one wanted in an out of the way storage box or be ruthless and discard. You do not need more than one photo to remember people or places.

- Saved photos can be sorted chronologically and/or by events such as vacations, weddings, etc.
- Shoe boxes or similar photo boxes can be used to store saved photos.
- File folders and boxes can be used to store regular size scrapbook papers. Larger papers can be stored in flat boxes or shallow drawers.
- Store small stickers and cut outs in plastic zip top bags or plastic page protectors.
- Use archival safe supplies for those photos you keep.
- Limit the number of papers and other supplies to a designated space. This may be a rolling tote, a shelf or cabinet. Apply the principle of only putting in a space what it will hold and no more.
- If upgrading to equipment or supplies with more features, sell or donate the equipment and supplies it replaces. Do not keep it just in case you might need it.
- Search online photo services and scrapbook dealers for more suggestions.

Card Making and Rubber Stamping

- Store papers in hanging file folders and boxes by color.
- Use shallow containers for rubber stamps and ink pads.
- Sort rubber stamps by categories when they are most often used: holidays, birthdays, etc.
- Save smaller pieces of papers, buttons, ribbons and other embellishments in zip top bags.
- Store smaller containers and other stamping supplies in larger totes or crates for portability and more convenient placement on shelves or in cabinets.

Sewing and Quilting

- Use a sewing table with adjustable legs so it can be lowered to a comfortable level while using the sewing machine.

- Divided plastic drawer sets and towers can be used to store notions and threads by color or type.

- Fabric can be folded on shelves or stored in bins or drawers.

- Sort fabrics by fiber content and/or color.

- Use one gallon zip top plastic bags for storing patterns.

- Store commercial patterns in file boxes designed for them or in size appropriate shoe boxes or plastic containers.

- Purge patterns and fabrics and sell or donate those you no longer use or like.

- Create a cutting and pressing table by placing a table on bed risers to make the height more back and neck friendly. Cover it with a padded board for pressing. A cutting mat can be placed on top of this as the need arises.

- Keep projects portable in the extra large zip top bags.

- Use rolling luggage or carts to move the sewing machine and other supplies to classes or out of the area temporarily.

Beading and Jewelry

- Sort beads by color or content.

- Sort beads in similar size and shaped containers so they can be stacked together.

- Consider fishing tackle boxes for sorting and storage of beads, wires and tools.

- Store stacks of containers on shelves in bookcases or cabinets with identifying labels on the front edge.
- Prevent beads from rolling off the work surface with a roll resistant mat or cover.

Painting Supplies

- Tackle boxes can be used to store small tubes of paint.
- Larger containers of paints are more accessible on shelving units.
- Brushes can be stored flat in shallow plastic bins, upright in tall cylinders or with paints in the bottom of large tackle boxes.
- Canvases and large painting surfaces can be stored upright in vertical storage slots or against a wall behind an easel or other stationery items.
- Easels that fold against the wall can allow for more movement in the space when they are not in use.
- Provide for good ventilation in areas where paints will be used.
- Remaining paint in brushes can be removed by rubbing the wet bristles back and forth across a bar of soap until the paint is forced out.
- Pallets containing paints can be covered with sealing wrap or placed in air tight bins and put in the freezer. This will keep them soft until they are needed again.

COLLECTIONS

We save things for many reasons and they all take up space. Anything you enjoy owning should be displayed for that enjoyment.

- Valuable collections such as rare coins or jewelry should be appraised, inventoried and stored in a safe place.

- Purge items you have collected but have no sentimental value and you do not want to display. See if a family member wants them before selling or donating.

- Have pictures taken of you with the item before removing it if you no longer have room for it.

- Limit the items you collect to the space that you have to display them. If you insist on storing some of them elsewhere, rotate them through your display so you can enjoy what you have.

- Group your collections together for the most attractive arrangements.

- The best collectible is money. Save it in interest bearing accounts rather than spending in on other items to collect. It takes no storage space and grows in value.

Storing Miscellaneous Items

- Save only very special greeting cards you have received. Cut off the verse and name of the giver to save and discard the front and envelope.

- If you purchase greetings cards for giving later on, store them in a decorative box on a shelf, in an accordion style file folder with appropriate labels or in file folders. They can also be put in tickler folders if you use those. These are labeled with days of the week and months of the year and are described further in Chapter 24.

- Make memories of sentimental items by creating shadow boxes, framed photo collages, pillow tops, album covers or quilts. These can be passed on to other generations.

- Make a child's craft kit by storing the supplies in a zip top big bag. Everything will be ready for them to use and clean up will be simple.

- Eliminate excessive gift wrapping supplies by investing in one or two rolls of paper. White or paper bag brown can be used for any occasion. They can be decorated with markers or rubber stamps or left plain with a pretty bow. Store in a flat container under the bed or in containers designed for them. Keeping one bright and one pastel roll of ribbon is sufficient.

- Use special ribbon holders if you maintain several rolls. These make it convenient for you to pull off one ribbon at a time.

Chapter 22

GUEST ROOMS AND FAMILY OFFICES

Singles, young couples without children and empty nesters often have a spare bedroom that can serve as a guest room. Some also have a spare room to use as an office for managing family affairs but others will have to use space in one of the occupied spaces to carry out these family items.

GUEST ROOM ORGANIZING PRINCIPLES

Guest rooms should be comfortable spaces that give visitors a place to rest and sleep while staying with you. Since the furnishings for it are simpler than other bedrooms, we will give simple suggestions for organizing that space.

This room may also have other functions when guests are not there. It could be the home office, a craft or sewing room, a play room for grandchildren or simply storage for items that would clutter other areas.

- Provide an adequate sleeping arrangement for your guests. This could be as simple as a sofa bed that is located in a multi purpose room or as elegant as a queen size brass bed. Regardless of the type, make sure the linens are clean and fresh.

- Clear the room of items that clutter it or that you may need while the guest is there.

- The room should have a door that closes for privacy.

- The window should have treatments that give privacy and block out light.

- There should be room for hanging clothing either on a rack or in a closet that has provided sufficient space. Provide plenty of hangers.

- Include a surface for opening the suitcase. It might be a table top, wide stool, ottoman or bench.

- Empty drawers let the guests know they are not intruders.

- Provide a chair for reading or just taking off shoes.

- A full length mirror is helpful even if it must be put on the back of the door.

- A small table or desk for writing is optional but may be an item that you use for storage, gift wrapping, etc. at other times. Adding paper, pens and other writing supplies is not necessary but nice touch.

- If there is not a separate bathroom for the guests, put out fresh towels and a basket of travel toiletries in the room. Fresh fruit, mints or chocolates can be added to make it extra special.

- Provide an alarm clock and lamp on a bedside table or chest.

- Extra blankets and pillows may be placed in the closet.

- Leave space around electrical outlets so they may be used for charging phones, etc. If that is not possible, attach a power strip to it to make plugs available.

Family Office/Management Space Organizing Principles

The family office or management space may be a designated room or a corner of the dining room, family room, bedroom or in a seldom used closet. Regardless of the space available, some basic organizing principles need to be considered.

If no area is available for separate office space or office furniture, consider using the dining room or kitchen table. All of the necessary supplies, files, etc. could be placed on rolling carts or portable totes that are stored elsewhere. This is not as convenient but can be a successful alternative when space is limited.

- Provide a writing surface for correspondence, writing checks and taking notes. This may be a table, a corner counter or standard style desk.

- Make provision for a computer. This could be a desktop model or laptop that takes less space.

- Label each end of cables and wires related to the computer and other electronic equipment. It will save much time in connecting or reconnecting.

- Use wire baskets that can be mounted under shelves or cable ties to contain wires.

- Consider replacing electronic items with wireless alternatives.

- Include a comfortable chair and good lighting.

- Office supplies such as paper, envelopes, paper clips, etc. can be stored in attractive containers on the writing surface if the space is large enough.

- Use drawers to contain supplies not stored on the writing surface. These may be part of the desk design or a free standing unit that is nearby or under a larger table.

- Filing supplies should be large enough to handle the family files. This may be file boxes for different categories of files, a cabinet with pull out drawers, or a rolling file trolley that can be stored in a closet when not in use. Refer to Chapter 11 for suggestions on managing papers.

- A telephone should be close at hand.

- If there is sufficient space, a bookcase for reference materials and other items is beneficial.

- If this office space is a convenient area to locate the family message center, consider placing those items in it. The best scenario would be to have them together in the most visited part of the house.

- If this space is in a more remote location, include containers for incoming and outgoing papers. This would include papers arriving from the incoming papers file box located in the more convenient place in the house.

- Regardless of its location, keep the surfaces clear before leaving it each time.

Platinum elfa Mesh File Cart

Chapter 23

HOME BUSINESS OFFICES

t his chapter has been placed between the family office/management area and organizing time and schedules because there are applications from each of those that apply to the home business. One significant difference is the space considerations.

Principles

- Contain identical or similar items together
- Put items used most often the closest to you. This usually means at or in your desk or work surface.
- Try to keep the work surface as clear as possible for working on projects.
- Create zones for each type of activity or function.

SPACE

If a home business will be used to consult clients or business associates, it should have a separate entrance from the outside or be located next to one of the existing entrances in the home. In existing homes where such an office was not planned, there may need to be some rearranging of rooms to accommodate the office. Creative planning can make this possible.

When there is no need for clients or associates to come to the office, then it can be located in another space that may be more suitable for the family and the person using the office. A spare bedroom, guest room, or portions of the family office/management area are options. Each of these has its pros and cons.

Spare Bedroom

The spare bedroom may be the best option if it will not be needed for any other purpose. Specific office furnishings can be placed in it and privacy would be provided. If there is the possibility of it being needed for another purpose in the future, multi-purpose furnishings such as a sofa bed may be a consideration.

Guest Room

A guest room would have some of the same benefits as a spare bedroom but it would not be available when guests arrive and the furnishings may be less office friendly. Multi-purpose furnishing are the best choice for using the room when guests are not there.

Family Office/Management Area

Using part of the family office/management area is an option if space in the house is limited. Care needs to be taken to separate the files, phone, and business supplies from those used for the family. If the family has a separate room for its office, this is usually not a problem.

If the family is using part of another room for its business/management, then placing the business office there also could create space problems. Finding another area may be more convenient.

Vacant Closet

If there is an open closet available, it can be transformed into a functional workspace. By taking out the closet rod and shelf and installing custom shelving, etc. you can have a comfortable work surface and storage area for supplies. When it is not in use, the door can be closed keeping the contents safe and out of site.

Platinum & Driftwood elfa Office in a Closet

Furnishings

Desk or Table

A sufficient workspace is needed for the business. It may be a desk or table but should provide room for writing, planning, a phone and possibly a computer station if there is not room for a separate station elsewhere. Do not clutter it with lots of little items.

If this will be shared with the family management area, the desk should contain drawers for business items only. When a table is used, drawer space can be provided by separate stacked drawer units that often have wheels for rolling into place when needed and out of the area for storage.

Modular Bamboo Drawer Organizers

Computer Station

Ideally a separate space for the computer will free up space on the desk for other paperwork and reading. A laptop computer is another option for added space. Such a station can be placed at a right angle to the desk to make access convenient or directly behind the desk if this arrangement works better in the room.

Chairs

Spending lots of time in a desk chair can be strenuous on the body. Choose an ergonomically designed chair that allows adjustment of height and support. It should have wheels and a comfortable seat.

If you will have clients or associates present, include two chairs that you can use for those meetings. It is not a friendly gesture to sit behind your desk when having discussions with someone else. These chairs can be as simple as straight backs with a padded cushion on the seat or fully upholstered chairs if there is adequate space.

Bookcase, Credenza or Table

Reference materials, printers, faxes, supplies, etc. need places to be stored. Decide on the type of furnishings that will fit in your space and accommodate your needs. Closets can often be used for storage of some items. Placing additional shelves or adding a small bookcase in the closet is one option for extra storage.

Credenzas and shorter bookcases will often fit under windows. And don't forget about overhead storage. Wall cabinets or shelves can be added for items that are not used as often. The same storage and display principles that apply to the rest of the house can apply in the office.

Files

The business should have separate file containers from those used by the family. It may be different drawers in a large file cabinet, file boxes that can be moved into the area as needed, or a rolling file trolley that is easily accessed.

As with family files, the business should have incoming paper files, action or project files and reference files. The incoming papers should have a file box on the desktop and the action or project files need to be in a desk drawer or other container close by. These are labeled specific to the business needs.

The reference files should be separate and can be stored further away than the others. Some older files should be boxed, labeled and stored elsewhere. It is becoming more common for older files to be scanned and stored in digital formats either locally or off site at online resources. Several of those options are listed in the resource section.

An outbox should also be included in the office. Papers that need to be copied, mail that needs to go out and items needed by someone else are examples of what can be placed in it.

Tickler files may be a good option for keeping up to date with the business schedule. These and other planners and calendars are discussed in Chapter 24.

Lighting

One of the most important but overlooked items in an office is the lighting. Our bodies are very light sensitive and the amount of good lighting can affect our moods as well as our ability to do work effectively. The nature of the work done in an office requires general as well as specific task lighting.

Windows are the best source for the perfect natural light they give, but allowing completely open views to the outside can cause distractions. Sheer curtains, blinds or shutters can be used to allow light in during the day and obstruct some of the view. They also give more privacy.

At night or in rooms with little natural light, general lighting can be created with ceiling fixtures or floor lamps. These spread light over a large area.

Task lighting is usually provided by lamps located on the table or desk and at other locations where reading, writing or other detailed work takes place. There are many styles and features available so that finding a lamp that is both functional and attractive is not a problem.

Technology

The business world is now deeply immersed in the technology arena and offices should be outfitted with those components that will make communication and processing documents effective. Computers with Internet access is a must as well as software that will provide the capabilities for data bases, e-mail accounts, word processing and accounting.

Fax machines, printers, copiers, scanners and a separate phone for the business should be considered, too. While there are some models that combine many of the functions into one piece of equipment, if there is sufficient space available, it is better to keep these items separate. If one part of the systems fails to function, you would still have other components working for you. All-in-one equipment can be used if space is limited and several components could not be placed in the office.

Office Supplies

Paper supplies make up a large part of an office. It is better to have most of those stored flat so edges do not get bent or folded. Stationary items, brochures and fact sheets are just some of these things that need a flat space for storage. Shallow drawers or literature racks can be used for these. Keep each item in a separate space and resist the urge to stack other working papers in them.

Keep the desk top as clear as possible. Contain only the items you will use on top of the desk or in the top drawer. Extra pens, paper clips, notepads, etc. can be store elsewhere.

A waste basket and shredder should be available as well as a clock and timer. These should be within easy access to the desk.

Some projects may require an extra table for putting together membership kits, marketing materials, etc. A folding table could be set up during those times to prevent the desk from being over run or cluttered. When the project is completed, the table can be removed and stored elsewhere.

PART FOUR
Solutions for Organizing Time

Chapter 24

TIME ORGANIZING TOOLS

h ave you ever forgotten a scheduled appointment or been late to pick up a child because you lost track of time? In our busyness we have come to depend on things that tell time and things that tell us how to use time. We will discuss some of those and how they might be used effectively.

BASIC TOOLS

Calendars provide a structure for us to organize our days, months and years and relate the time we spend with others. We set doctor's appointments, parent-teacher conferences, vacations, etc. with mutual calendars in hand. Calendars alone cannot help us organize our time but we should invest in those that are most effective for our lifestyle.

Planners have calendars but offer space for including more details. They can include spaces for additional information such as task lists, contact information, and long range planning. These are used to actually plan and organize you time. It is difficult to organize your time most effectively without one.

Master Calendars

Families need a calendar that includes activities and appointments for everyone in the family. This helps to prevent overlapping commitments and trying to be two places at once.

- A large wall calendar in a message center or prominent place that all can see works well for writing in scheduled events. Color codes can be used for certain activities or people in the family. Details of events can be recorded and saved in the Household Notebook discussed in Chapter 11.

  It is a good idea to write the information in pencil so changes can be easily made if needed.

- A portable wall calendar. These are calendars that can be folded and carried away from the wall. They have spaces for reoccurring appointments and activities so there is no need for 12 large monthly pages to record information. The resource section of this book has contact information to learn more about them.

- Computer software that uses calendars and scheduling can have necessary information recorded and printed copies can be made and displayed. These are not as large as the typical wall calendar.

  If all of the family members use the computer daily, it may be a good option. Individual computers in the household can be networked so everyone sees the same calendar information.

Personal Calendars

In order to keep the master calendars up to date, members of the family who do the scheduling, make appointments, etc. need a portable calendar to carry with them most of the time.

- Pocket Calendars are small calendars that usually let you view one month at a time. Significant events can be written in them but there is not much room for details.

- A slightly larger version of this is the desk calendar. They come in several sizes but are not as convenient to carry with you unless you normally have a large purse or briefcase. It can have monthly, weekly or daily views depending on the size and style and allow for additional writing space.

Planners

- Notebook planners are usually spiral or ring binders with pages that can be added or removed. They come in several sizes but are never as small as pocket calendars. Each may have a daily or weekly calendar view but it is divided into time slots. They normally include a monthly and yearly calendar and other helpful planning tools. You can customize the ring binders with task lists, contact information and more.

  Because there is so much detail in them, they are somewhat bulky and difficult to carry unless you use a briefcase. If these are your preference, there are many styles, cover choices and options for you to add. Shop for one that best suits your needs and tastes.

- Electronic planners or PDAs contain the same information options as notebooks but are small devices run by batteries. They are more convenient to carry and store all types of information but it takes time to learn how to use them. The more they are used the more frequently you must charge them, but once a day is sufficient.

  Some styles have the capability of having their information stored in and retrieved from computer programs. They can be updated from the PDA or computer and syncing the information between the two takes less than a minute. This provides a back up source of all information.

The calendar program can store reoccurring events, can be viewed by day, week, or month and can be printed in each of the views. Other information can be printed as needed.

- Some wireless phones can store the electronic information from the planner computer programs. This enables you to have your PDA and phone together in one device and sync it into you computer for updates each way. These are the most expensive but the most versatile of all the planners.

Reminder or Tickler Files

These files were first introduced in business offices as a means of keeping up with information needed for appointments, clients, etc. They have made their way into busy homes as a means of keeping up with information in a timely manner.

The files have folders or sections for each day of the month and a separate set for each month of the year. Information and reminders are stored in the monthly sections and at the beginning of each month is transferred into the appropriate day of the month for that activity. Each day you should check to see the reminders and information you will need and then return it to the monthly folder. You would repeat this at the beginning of every month.

- There are several options for these files described below.
- Hanging file folders can be used that are labeled with the days of the month in the front and the months of the year in the back. Information is dropped into the appropriate folder.
- Accordion style pocket files are available in most office supply store that contain separate sections for each day and month. These are portable

and an option if you do not have enough space for hanging folders or want to have your files with you at home when you leave home.

- PDAs and phones with PDA capability have built in reoccurring and daily task features. Some have actual pop up windows that can remind you of the event or task to be done. These can be set to remind you as far ahead as you set it and continue to remind you in time increments until you dismiss it. It can be more than a tickler: it can be a nag if you set it that way.

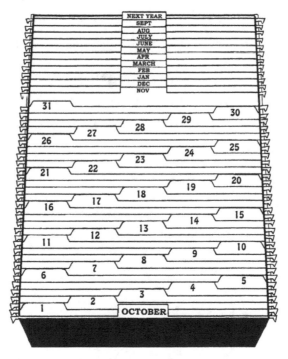

Hanging Folder Tickler Files

Contact Lists

There should be a complete list of all the personal, professional and business contacts in a central place for all to see. This should include names, addresses, phone numbers and any other important information.

- Address books can be used for storing this information. The best style is one that has removable pages that can be deleted as information changes or added when more contact information is needed.

- File cards on flipping or rolling trays or in a file box are convenient to use and the cards can be added and removed easily. They are not as portable as the address book but allow for lots of information to be written on the card.

- Household Notebooks can have a section for contacts but the large pages may not be as easily changed when more current information is needed. These notebooks are ideal places for often used contact information such as health providers, local take out restaurants, school, church or committee rosters.

- Electronic data bases provide the most versatile uses of contact information. Some computer software data can be downloaded into PDAs and some phones so the information is portable as well as available in one place for access by all family members. Updates and current contact information is easily maintained and can be printed if desired.

Household Notebooks

These were mentioned in Chapter 11 but they need to be identified as a time organizing tool because they can contain information that saves time. Any schedules, rosters, activity or household information can be kept in them for quick access.

If there is a paper you continually use, keep it protected and convenient in this notebook. It may also store lists of reoccurring events, household maintenance schedules, family chore charts, meals and lists of reminders for trips, holiday shopping, etc. Finding these quickly is a time saver.

A resource for more information in using them is listed in the resource section.

Project Folders

Keeping a separate folder or file jacket for current projects is the best way to keep all relevant information about the project together. These folders should be close at hand and are often called hot files in an office setting. It is beneficial to have a time tracking calendar or chart at the front to be sure you are on schedule. You can drop any notes, reminders, assignments, etc. in them to be included in the final product.

Assistance

One of the best but most overlooked time organizing tools is other people. Family members should each have responsibilities in the home. Chore schedules can be given to even very young children. It makes them feel a part of the family, teaches them responsibility and self confidence.

You and your spouse may have established chore guidelines when you first married but the arrival of children and/or two parents working may have changed the dynamics of those guidelines. Each partner must be flexible in getting the needed tasks done. If there is continual conflict about responsibilities, I suggest a qualified counselor mediate the situation. I am serious and I will leave it at that.

If finances allow it, some tasks can be hired out. Use reputable sources and be specific in your expectations.

Bartering or sharing tasks with friends or using project groups discussed in Chapter 7 is another option. Sometimes menial tasks can be more fun with friends. Taking turns babysitting and chauffeuring kids to activities can be a way to arrange your schedule for larger blocks of time to complete projects.

Notepads

Keep a small spiral or other bound notepad with you at all times. This allows you to jot down information without losing it. Sticky notes may work at your desk or near the phone, but notepads are a safer and more flexible way to keep the information.

Regardless of how you take down the information, transfer it into a permanent location on a daily basis.

Chapter 25

TIME ORGANIZING SYSTEMS

every personality type has its own preference when it comes to organizing their time. You will need to develop your own system but there are some guiding principles that all good systems need. These go back to some of the basic organizing principles discussed in Chapters 5 and 6.

- **Priorities in your life must be included in any schedule.** Just like you need to think over your priorities before you plan spaces, you need to think about what you want to do in you life before you plan schedules. You should include small and large projects and short and long term goals. Whether it is painting the bathroom or organizing the garage, reading a book or finishing a college degree, they will never get done unless you identify what is important for you to do.

  These must be included in any planning or scheduling and should be written down on paper or in your computer where they can remind you as you plan your time. Failure to consider your goals in planning is a guarantee there will be no time for them. Keep them in focus throughout the week

- **Break down larger projects and long term goals into smaller tasks** that can be included in your plans. It may be as simple as choosing the color for the bathroom or calling for a college course schedule.

  You may use the old style of outlining the project or goal beginning with the larger tasks listed and then breaking down each of those into smaller and smaller segments.

  Or you may use the more contemporary method of mind mapping used in most schools today. Start with the largest task in the center and create spokes from it for the smaller task. Even smaller segments can be added under those.

  Regardless of your method take those priorities, goals and projects and break them down into small manageable tasks and create a plan to get them done.

- **Planning and Planners are part of the time organizing strategy.** Find a suitable time for you to plan and choose a planner style that works for you. Try not to jump around from one planner to the next as an excuse for not organizing your time. Just be sure the planner contains hourly time increments for each day.

  You will never be able to accomplish what you really want to do unless you train yourself to set aside a time to plan your activities and have a planner ready to put the activities in their place.

- **Understanding how long it takes to do certain tasks** is important in planning your time. You may be surprised that some mental tasks involve much more time than you would estimate. Other daily chores may take half the time you thought since they are routine and almost automatic.

Using a timer to determine just how long it takes for most of the things you do is a good way to get more into your schedule. Try timing how long it takes to fold a load of laundry, unload the dishwasher, read and answer e-mail, take a child to soccer practice or take out the trash.

I am sure you have already timed how long it takes to get to work or other routes you frequently travel. If you have a good idea how long it takes to do your other routine activities, you will be able to find more hours in your day.

SCHEDULING SYSTEMS

Creating a system that works for you may be a trial and error process for a while but you will be able to create a rhythm that works for you once you get started using the tools and commit to the process. Give each system a couple of weeks before you decide to move on to another one.

Large Project Planning

- Activities like holidays, vacations, yard sales, etc. require planning well in advance of the event. Just like other priorities and goals, they should be broken down into manageable tasks and scheduled.
- Put the date of the event on the calendar and schedule the tasks that need to be done in reverse order at some point on the monthly and weekly calendars. You may want to put a shopping day for

the Thanksgiving dinner a week ahead or calling the out of town campground or hotel months ahead of the vacation.

- Check off the tasks as you get them done and adjust the list as needed.

Weekly planning

- It is a good idea to make some plans at the beginning of each week and then create a daily schedule as the week progresses. Monthly activities are normally on the calendar in advance so most planning is done on a weekly and/or daily basis.

- In your planner block out the activities that have already been scheduled for that week. If there is an appointment that requires travel, allow 15 minutes additional travel time for traffic and/or parking problems.

- Reoccurring appointments such as weekly church attendance or daily baseball practice for Johnny should be blocked out, too.

- Block out any personal time you have on a reoccurring basis at a specific time such as working out at the gym or choir rehearsal.

- List routine tasks that are done on a regular basis. If there is a specific time such as family time every day or a special date with your spouse on Friday evening, include them on the schedule. If it is laundry on Monday and Thursday or meal preparation times put those in the appropriate day but allow for flexibility in the time slot.

- Include leisure activities for you and your family. These are as important as any household task but don't need to be all consuming. Use common sense and wisdom to find a balance.

- Now the fun comes. Look at your breakdown of projects and goals you created from your priorities exercise and list one or more of those as activities for each day. This is the only way you will ever get them done. You may think you will never get around to them but you must plan for them. You are simply creating a plan to do more than you ever have done in those same 24 hours.

- Allow flexibility in your schedule and don't let an unraveling of events throw you off. Life happens and activities can take more time than you thought or emergencies can throw the entire day or week out the window. Regroup and adjust the schedule as necessary. Be careful not to give up on what you want to do, but pick up the planner and make changes that will get you back on track.

Daily Planning

- Plan your day the night before or first thing in the morning if you are an early riser. This should be done in the planner. If you plan at night, you can also put out clothing, lunches, backpacks, etc. for the next day so there is less panic in the morning.

- Check your planner to see if any adjustments need to be made to the schedule. If there were unexpected delays or new items, take care to reorder the day to make room for those.

- Group activities, appointments and necessary routines together as much as makes sense. If you are the car pool driver this week, combine the other errands that need to be done while you are in the car. If you are doing the laundry, pick up the trash or vacuum the floor while the washer or dryer is running.

- Dovetail as many tasks on your list that you can but do not add other activities that might take you off your schedule. Do not multi-task thinking activities, only routine chores. This takes planning or you will find yourself wasting time.

- Use your biological clock to schedule the most challenging tasks when you are at your best. We all have those times when we have more energy, are most creative and productive. Use those times to their greatest advantage. Schedule dentist appointments, routine activities and less difficult jobs at the down times.

- Block out down time everyday near the other activities. A 30 minute nap is a good idea if you are frequently staying up late helping with a teenager's homework. Spending time reviewing the day with a spouse is time well spent. You may choose to read or write in a journal, but you need to allow yourself time to breathe. This does not mean you take a 3 hour nap or watch television all evening. You get the picture.

- After this planning is done, you will see some small blocks of time remaining on some days and larger blocks of time on other days. Put those projects and/or goal tasks that you chose for the week in those time blocks. The larger blocks should have the largest task. Do not allow that time to be filled with other busyness.

- It may look like you have not left any time for a shoelace to break, but have no fear, you are making the most of your day. When you see that you have actually accomplished some of those tasks on your priorities list, it will give you the motivation to stick with the system.

- Again, follow the plan and if it falls apart, regroup without frustration. Keep the system in place and adjust as necessary.

- Create a task or To Do list for the day after the schedule is in place. This can be done in the planner or on a separate schedule and is the details of the scheduled activities. The car pool may have a list of which children to pick up, the appointment may have the phone number or directions, the errands may include the grocery list and which book to get at the library. Whatever the details, include them.

If you have grocery or similar lists that have been building for several days, attach them to the To Do list.

- As you go through the day, check off the accomplished tasks and make adjustments where you need them.

- Be careful not to add activities you have not planned unless it is urgent or most important at that time. Do not get sidetracked on things you may think need to be done. Losing your focus and adding in activities that are not on your schedule can cause you to lose the time to do those priority tasks. Doing trivial tasks that you did not plan in order to avoid the more important things is a form of procrastination.

- Do not multi-task activities that require you to think. Brain studies have shown there are changes in your brain functions when you incorporate extra activities in the thinking process. Focusing on one thing at a time develops concentration skills so necessary for problem solving and decision making. Even eliminating background noise that we love so much like television or radio helps the focusing skills.

Chapter 26

Preventing Lost and Wasted Time

busyness and bad habits can cause you to lose or waste time that was available to allow you to reach your goals and make the most important things the most important things you do. Being aware of the time devouring traps is as important as doing the planning.

Time wasting traps can rob you of spending your time where you planned to spend it and distract you from what you want and planned to do. Most of these are very subtle and some are very good things that make you feel good about doing them but they should be avoided unless they were planned.

Over Scheduling-Part I

Learn to say no. Do not volunteer for or take on more than you can handle. If you absolutely love to do certain things or have a passion in some area, then put that on your priorities list and make room for it. Volunteering for those things will make your life full and be a blessing to others.

Too many times your willingness to help out in areas you love is interpreted as a willingness to volunteer for anything. Be firm in your commitment to make your time work for you and your family and resist the requests to help anyone anywhere with anything.

I personally believe you need to create a generic "saying no" statement that you memorize and repeat to any offers you cannot accept, do not want to accept or should not accept. Here is mine.

"Thank you so much for thinking of me but I am not able to do that. I hope you will find someone who can help you, and if I think of anyone I will let you know. I appreciate your confidence in me but I must say no."

Be sure to repeat the word "no" in every following sentence if they try to press you with how little time it will take or that you will have help, etc.

"That is thoughtful of you, but I must say no."
"I am sure that would be a big help, but I must say no."
"I know this would be a wonderful opportunity, but I must say no."
"Yes, it is an important event, but I must say no."

I think you get the drift. Honestly you must practice this in order to stay on guard and be ready. After a while it will be second nature and you will get fewer and fewer calls or requests for help.

Realize you do not have to give a reason for saying no. See the request as a thief trying to get in your schedule and steal time just like one would come into your house and steal your things. It sounds brutal, but your time is precious, you only have so much of it and it will be gone if you don't use it like a good steward.

If you are overcome with guilt, the Online Organizing web site listed in the resource section has an article by Ramona Creel on 20 ways to say no.

These are legitimate excuses, but try to understand that you really do not need a reason to turn down a thief.

Over Scheduling Part II

Learn to say no to personal and family activities that cannot realistically fit into your schedule. There are so many good things you or your children will want to do but cannot be fit into a normal person's schedule. If you really are trying to be super-human or super-parent or trying to prove something to somebody including yourself, you can attempt to work them in, but I don't recommend it for sanity's sake. Go back to your priorities and see if these activities are included in reaching your goals.

Our environments have provided us with endless opportunities to have fun, improve our health, learn new things and practice those skills we already have. There are endless teams and sports for us and our children, courses of study to take to enhance our lives, but there are not enough hours in our day or week to fit in everything that would be good or beneficial to us.

When you have established a routine and schedule that works with your present activities, you may find there is time for more of the things you have wanted to do. The same may be true for children. Until then, it may be better to wait and see if there are any available time slots for more activities.

I can almost promise you that lost opportunities now will not be lost forever. Hang in there, be patient and don't give up hope or become frustrated or feel deprived. New activities are always coming around and there will be time in the future for some of those.

Procrastinating

It is easy to find an excuse if we don't want to do something. We can fill our days with trivial tasks rather than working on more difficult projects. We can look busy and get a few things done, but we will never reach our goals that way or get those bigger projects done.

If perfectionism is keeping you from working on those tasks, remember doing something is always better than doing nothing and the results are often better than we imagined. Breaking the projects and goals down into manageable tasks as discussed earlier makes it seem less threatening and eliminates the "all or nothing" thinking. Once you get started, you will be motivated to continue as you as you are rewarded with what has been accomplished.

Television Distractions

With a television in nearly every room of the house and the habit of always having news, entertainment and information around us, it is difficult to create an environment without it. We get attached to certain programs and even plan our lives around them.

The media has created programs to attract you to itself and distract you from anything else. If you are a visual learner or your brain is most attracted by sight, it will be difficult for you to concentrate on the tasks at hand if the television is on. Even with the best of intentions and plans, you can lose or waste much time watching when you should be busy with what you planned to do.

Some people can listen to the radio, tapes or CDs without as much distraction. If you must have some type of entertainment or sound as you work, consider listening rather than watching television. If you are working on difficult tasks or the job requires creative or logical thinking to be completed, less distraction from any noise is better for getting the job done correctly.

Computer Overuse

The lowering costs of computers and the increase in software applications and games for the computers have made them an attractive way to spend our time. They have also been able to absorb more and more of our time. There is no doubt they have improved our lives in many ways, but they have also provided the temptation to waste time. In order to keep our schedules and lives in balance, limits must be set on their use.

E-mail messages at home and work need to be checked only 2-3 times a day. Resist the forwarded messages as non-essential reading and delete or move them to a folder designated for leisure reading.

Never forward messages you have not read especially if they are warnings. Always check those out for yourself even if they say they have been checked. This takes even more valuable time and is why I recommend you do not read them. Signing on to more than one e-mail account as discussed earlier will help eliminate lots of messages from commercial and non-essential senders.

Reply to those messages that require a response and make your message brief. E-mail is not the place for long letters. Phone calls are often a better choice when lots of information or details are needed. Create folders for saving messages you consider important or print them if you must. Resist the urge to print everything. It can create more clutter.

Searching or surfing the Internet should be limited to a specific time in the schedule and for a specific duration. I recommend shopping online rather than walking the malls, but you should limit it to what is on your needs list.

A great reminder item is the Time Timer that will keep track of the remaining time you have to spend at the computer. You can purchase it as software or a stand alone timer. It is listed in the resource section. Regardless of the type of timer you use, it is a good idea to set one every time you sit down at a computer.

Distracting Tasks

It never fails that you will see something else that needs to be done while you are working on a project you planned. Unless it can be done in less than a minute, resist the urge to get distracted from what you are doing. There are always more things that need to be done than you can do in a day or maybe even a lifetime. Stick to your plan and get the most out of your time by doing what you planned to do. In the long run, you will accomplish more of those things than if you get sidetracked.

Distracting People

The best made plans can be flushed down the drain if your schedule is interrupted by unexpected visits, phone calls or pushy people. Using voice mail to accept calls when you are working on difficult tasks is the best use of your time. If you must take the call, try using the hands free phone sets.

Impromptu visits can be reduced by planning face to face meetings with people who may drop by.

If you need uninterrupted time, tell those who may distract you in advance what you are doing. When my daughter-in-law began home schooling my oldest grandchild, she sent a message to everyone explaining the hours she would be teaching and asked not to be disturbed during that time. She lets phone messages go to the voice mail and only checks her e-mail messages after those hours. She keeps a separate contact number for emergencies only. Planning ahead can eliminate lots of distractions.

Over Reading

We read for pleasure but for information also. In spite of the multitude of television channels that can tell us anything we want to know, we order magazines, newsletters and get books to read. Not everything printed is important and learning to skim information is a good skill. If you enjoy leisure reading, then schedule that time for yourself, but don't get distracted by every piece of literature that comes into the house.

Waiting Time

If the rest of the world would learn to schedule as accurately as we can, we would never have to wait again. But alas, there will be times when we are required to sit and wait, or God forbid, stand and wait. Be prepared.

While waiting in the car you can listen to books on CDs or make those phone calls on your "To Do" list. While sitting in an waiting room, you can write notes for the next day, catch up on correspondence or read.

Be prepared for such events. I carry needlework in my car and only work on the projects when I have to sit and wait. It took me 11 years to finish my last project but it was worth it. I have a large, framed traditional sampler now hanging on my family room wall. I have visual proof my waiting time was not wasted and you can too.

Stress and Fatigue

Being anxious and tired are deterrents to getting things done. No matter how much you plan, when you are sick or not at your best you don't want to work. A balanced diet, exercise and rest are all important in overcoming stress and fatigue.

Depression, hormonal imbalances, and other health problems can be causes of those feelings and should be treated by medical professionals. If you cannot find the problems that are causing your distress, then do not hesitate to see out medical treatment.

Maintenance

More things mean more time to take care of them. Limit the stuff and you eliminate lots of time consuming maintenance.

Some items require more care than similar items. Silver bowls must be polished but crystal bowls do not and they both are elegant. Lots of little frames require more time in dusting than one large frame with a divided mat for lots of pictures.

Tables covered with fabrics require less cleaning than dusting and polishing wood tops. Small objects contained in a tray or basket makes cleaning around that one thing easier than cleaning around each object. Think and plan ahead when making purchases so you have more time for yourself and spend less time on things.

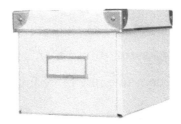

FINAL THOUGHTS

SOPHIE WAS DISTRESSED because we did not finish organizing her home office in one morning. In fact, it took two additional mornings to get the job done. Disorganization doesn't happen overnight and it will take more than just an hour or two getting it back in shape.

One of the most eye opening things about getting organized is the understanding that it is a process and not an event. If surroundings are cluttered, it will take time to declutter the space and then establish an organizational plan that will help maintain it. If a schedule is so full there is no time for leisure or relationships, then getting back on track will take trial and error in planning before there is progress.

Unlike the microwave, organizing time is measured in hours and days not seconds and minutes. Patience and consistency are the most important attitudes in finding success in making your space and time the best they can be. But when you see the results, you will feel freedom from things that took so much of your peace. And you will be able to enjoy the freedom to relax in a schedule that allows for reaching your goals and spending time with those you love.

Being organized gives you free time resulting from not having to hunt for lost or misplaced items. Your finances are free to invest in the future rather than in duplicate or lost items. You have freedom from clutter conflicts in your relationships and you set an example for those around you. You are free from the guilt and embarrassment you feel when visitors arrive in your cluttered space. Getting organized sets you free.

Yes, there are more important things than being organized, but being organized gives us the freedom to enjoy those important things. Choose to be free.

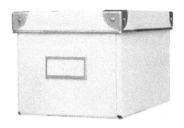

ORGANIZING RESOURCES

CDs

By Mary Frances Ballard: available by e-mail or through her web site:

www.orderlyplaces.com

maryfrances@orderlyplaces.com

Staging Your Home for a Quick Sale

Moving Out and Moving In Helpful Hints

Organizing to Make Cleaning Quick and Easy

Holiday Organizing Tips and Tricks

Books

By Don Aslett: Entertaining and easy to read; my organizing guru:

Clutter's Last Stand

Lose 200 LBS This Weekend

How to Have a 48 Hour Day

To better understand the mental or emotional influences in disorganization:

Making Peace with the Things in Your Life, Cindy Glovinsky

Buried in Treasures, David Tolin

Messie No More, Sandra Felton

Other books:

Simplify Your Life, Marcia Ramsland, Women of Faith

Taming the Paper Tiger at Home, Barbara Hemphill

Organizing for Dummies, Eileen Roth

Organizing Plain and Simple, Donna Smallin

The Organizing Sourcebook, Kathy Waddill

Organizing from the Inside Out, Julie Morgenstern

Websites *(Accurate as of this publishing date)*

http://organizingtipsfromorderlyplaces.blogspot.com/

Orderly Places organizing blog

www.organizedhome.com

free printable notebook forms, good solutions

www.onlineorganizing.com

more organizing tips

www.findmyorganizer.com

resource for locating local professional organizers

www.napo.net

National Association of Professional Organizers

www.nsgcd.org

National Study Group on Chronic Disorganization with information
on hoarding

www.thecontainerstore.com

organizing products

www.organize-everything.com

organizing products

www.scandigital.com

    source for scanning and storing photos digitally

www.pixily.com

    source for scanning and storing all types of files

www.allrecipes.com

    recipes by topic or ingredients

www.foodnetwork.com

    recipes from chefs around the world

www.timetimer.com

    software and stand alone timer and reminder

www.snopes.com

    used to verify e-mail alerts, stories, etc.

http://urbanlegends.about.com/

    used to verify e-mail alerts, stories, etc.

www.donotcall.gov/

    to remove your phone numbers from telemarketers

http://www.salvationarmysouth.org/valueguide.htm

    donation values

http://www.goodwillwm.org/donate/estimatedvalues.html

    donation values

www.weekdate.com

    flexible and portable planners and calendars

www.thefamilyorganizer.com

    planners and calendars for organizing families

To remove your name from junk mailing lists

Make one master copy with the names of everyone at your address in every form (John Paul, John P. J. P. etc.), your address and request to be removed and send it to the addresses below.

Direct Marketing Association, Inc.

1120 Avenue of the Americas

New York, NY 10036-6700

You may also use their web site to go through the same process.

http://www.dmachoice.org

And, of course you may contact me for organizing assistance, speaking engagements or more information:

maryfrances@orderlyplaces.com

www.orderlyplaces.com

http://organizingtipsfromorderlyplaces.blogspot.com/

757-806-4008

Or

Morgan James Publishing LLC

1-800-485-4943

1225 Franklin Avenue, Suite 325

Garden City, NY 11530-1693

ABOUT THE AUTHOR

WHEN MARY FRANCES BALLARD'S MOTHER told her to clean up her room, she could have never imagined it would lead to her becoming a professional organizer. But that is exactly what happened. It did take a few more lessons, many more years and considerable metamorphosis but today she is living proof of the power of a mother's persuasion.

As a professional organizer, Mary Frances owns Orderly Places a business whose mission is to encourage, assist and educate others in organizing solutions. She is a member of the National Association of Professional Organizers, the National Study Group on Chronic Disorganization and Faithful Organizers

As a public speaker she presents programs and workshops to business organizations, libraries, churches, garden clubs and other community groups with humor and practical applications that even a spouse can understand. Using her experiences as a classroom teacher, wife, mother and grandmother, she appeals to all age groups, sexes and species.

Her serious identity includes being a Newport News, Virginia native and a graduate of James Madison University with degrees in Home Economics

and Education. In her leisure time, she is a quilter and has written and led
Bible Studies. She and her husband, Eddie, live in Newport News with their
border collie, Kasey.

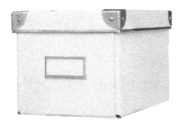

PRESENTATIONS FOR YOUR ORGANIZATION

MARY FRANCES BALLARD has been speaking to business, community and church organizations with enthusiasm, information and humor for many years. She is available for programs, workshops and seminars. Her presentations will inspire and motivate your group members so they will be ready to make positive changes their lives. More information may be found at her website or through e-mail.

www.orderlyplaces.com
maryfrances@orderlyplaces.com

A SELECTION OF PRESENTATIONS, LECTURES AND WORKSHOPS

Fun filled, interactive and motivating, these presentations can be customized to suit you group's interests, needs and time allotments.
Contact us for more information and scheduling.

Save Yourself (and others, too)—Solutions for saving time, space, money and other resources by being organized are examined in a humorous presentation.

Money in the Mail or Mail Madness? –Develop a paper flow system to keep important items from getting misplaced in the stacks of papers arriving daily.

Money Saving Organizational Tools—Before spending hard earned money on specialized organizing supplies and tools, learn how to make the most of everyday household items you already have to organize your spaces.

De-clutter Your Head and House—Unused items in your house are taking up valuable space there and in your brain, too. Learn ways to free up your mind, time, money and resources as you prioritize those things around you.

How the Virtuous Woman Got So Much Done—A Biblical and Christian approach to personal and home organization using *the 5 P's of Orderly Places*™. This is also available in half day and all day workshops.

Organizing Your Head, Heart and House—An organizing look at keeping balance in your body, mind and spirit as well as your house.

Time Stretcher: One Hour Organizing—Strategies are presented to make your house presentable but not perfect in just a few minutes.

Let There Be Music, not Madness—Organizing solutions for Music Teachers.

Saving Time and More—A look at time management for work schedules, everyday tasks and the things we want to work into our busy lives

Economize--Organize—See your space from a different perspective and learn how to save money and use effective organizing strategies.

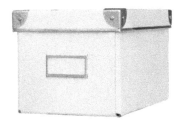

BONUS

THANK YOU FOR PURCHASING THIS BOOK. We hope you enjoyed the organizing strategies included and as a bonus for your purchase we now make available to you a CD titled *Organizing Tips for Holidays and Special Events*.

To receive your free CD, e-mail us: maryfrances@orderlyplaces.com

We will respond with information so that you may receive your copy.

BUY A SHARE OF THE FUTURE IN YOUR COMMUNITY

These certificates make great holiday, graduation and birthday gifts that can be personalized with the recipient's name. The cost of one S.H.A.R.E. or one square foot is $54.17. The personalized certificate is suitable for framing and will state the number of shares purchased and the amount of each share, as well as the recipient's name. The home that you participate in "building" will last for many years and will continue to grow in value.

Here is a sample SHARE certificate:

YES, I WOULD LIKE TO HELP!

I support the work that Habitat for Humanity does and I want to be part of the excitement! As a donor, I will receive periodic updates on your construction activities but, more importantly, I know my gift will help a family in our community realize the dream of homeownership. **I would like to SHARE in your efforts against substandard housing in my community!** *(Please print below)*

PLEASE SEND ME _____ SHARES at $54.17 EACH = $ $_____

In Honor Of: _____

Occasion: (Circle One)   HOLIDAY   BIRTHDAY   ANNIVERSARY

       OTHER: _____

Address of Recipient: _____

Gift From: _____ *Donor Address:* _____

Donor Email: _____

I AM ENCLOSING A CHECK FOR $ $_____ PAYABLE TO HABITAT FOR HUMANITY <u>OR</u> PLEASE CHARGE MY VISA OR MASTERCARD *(CIRCLE ONE)*

Card Number _____ Expiration Date: _____

Name as it appears on Credit Card _____ Charge Amount $ _____

Signature _____

Billing Address _____

Telephone # Day _____ Eve _____

PLEASE NOTE: Your contribution is tax-deductible to the fullest extent allowed by law.
Habitat for Humanity • P.O. Box 1443 • Newport News, VA 23601 • 757-596-5553
www.HelpHabitatforHumanity.org

Printed in the USA
CPSIA information can be obtained
at www.ICGtesting.com
JSHW082153140824
68134JS00014B/216